LARRY SANG'S

CHINESE ASTROLOGY & FENG SHUI GUIDE

2010

The Year of The Tiger

with Lorraine Wilcox

LARRY SANG'S

The Year of the Tiger

ASTROLOGY AND FENG SHUI GUIDE

Original Title:
Master Larry Sang's 2010 The Year of the Tiger, Astrology and Feng Shui Guide

Published by: The American Feng Shui Institute
111 N. Atlantic Blvd, Suite 352
Monterey Park, CA 91754. U.S.A.
Email: fsinfo@amfengshui.com
www.amfengshui.com

Written by:
Master Larry Sang

Edited by:
Lorraine Wilcox

Layout by:
Afriany Simbolon

Calligraphy by Larry Sang

*Aging can be moderated
if one takes a light view
of fame and wealth.
Virtual immortality can
be achieved if one is free
of wants and worries*

Please Read This Information

This book provides information regarding the subject matter covered. The authors are not engaged in rendering legal, medical or other professional advice. If you need medical or legal advice, a competent professional should be contacted. Chinese Astrology and Feng Shui are not get-rich-quick or cure-all schemes. Changes in your life will happen as fast as you are ready for them. Be patient in your study of Chinese Astrology and Feng Shui.

The authors have tried to make this book as complete and accurate as possible. However, there may be typographical or content mistakes. Use this book as a general guide in your study of Chinese Astrology and Feng Shui

This book was written to educate and entertain. The authors, distributors and the American Feng Shui Institute shall have neither liability nor responsibility to any person with respect to any loss or damage caused, or alleged to be caused by this book.

The following pages of predictions will help you understand trends as they develop through the coming year. Please keep in mind that they are somewhat general because other stellar influences are operative, according to the month, date and exact minute of your birth. Unfortunately, we cannot deal with each person individually in this book.

Table of Contents

Calligraphy by
Larry Sang

老年人相信一切
中年人懷疑一切
年青人什麼都懂

The old believe everything;
the middle-aged doubt everything;
the young know everything

How to find your Animal Sign

In order to find your correct animal sign, as well as understand why the Chinese calendar begins in February, and not January, it is important to have a little understanding of the two different Chinese calendars. As with most things Chinese, we look at the Yin and Yang. In Chinese timekeeping, there is a Yin calendar (lunar calendar) and a Yang calendar (solar calendar).

The Lunar Calendar

The Lunar Calendar is perhaps the best known and most popular of the two. Chinese Lunar New Year is frequently celebrated with a lot of pageantry. It is used in one type of Chinese astrology called Zi Wei Dou Shu, and also in Yi-Jing calculations.

The Solar Calendar

The Solar calendar is less well known. The early Chinese meteorologists attempted to gain insight into the cycles of the seasons. From this study, they developed the Solar calendar. This calendar is used in the form of Chinese Astrology called Four Pillars, as well as in Feng Shui. The Chinese were very accurate in their studies. Without computers, and using only observations, they mapped a solar year of 365 days. They missed the actual timing of a year by only 14 minutes and 12 seconds.

The solar year is divided into 24 solar terms. Each lasts about fifteen days. Spring Begins (lichun) is the name of the first day of spring, and the first solar term. It is exactly midway between the winter solstice and the spring equinox. This is why it always falls on February 4th or 5th. We begin the five elements with wood, so the Chinese New Year begins with a wood month, whether in the Lunar or the Solar calendar. These concepts are derived from the Yi-Jing.

How to find your Animal Sign

To find your animal sign, start with your birth date. If it is before February 4th (Spring Begins), use the prior year for the Chinese calendar. If it is after February 4th, then use the same birth year. If it is on February 4th, then you need the time of the birth to accurately determine the birth animal. This information is contained in the Chinese Ten-Thousand Year Calendar. (The American Feng Shui Institute has one available as an ebook at www.amfengshui.com). In the following pages, the birth years are listed for each animal, but remember, if your birthday is before February 4th, use the previous year to determine the animal.

The Twelve Animals

Rat 鼠	Ox 牛	Tiger 虎	Rabbit 兔
1924, 1936, 1948, 1960, 1972, 1984, 1996, 2008	1925, 1937, 1949, 1961, 1973, 1985, 1997, 2009	1926, 1938, 1950, 1962, 1974, 1986, 1998, 2010	1927, 1939, 1951, 1963, 1975, 1987, 1999
Dragon 龍	Snake 蛇	Horse 馬	Sheep 羊
1928, 1940, 1952, 1964, 1976, 1988, 2000	1929, 1941, 1953, 1965, 1977, 1989, 2001	1930, 1942, 1954, 1966, 1978, 1990, 2002	1931, 1943, 1955, 1967, 1979, 1991, 2003
Monkey 猴	Rooster 雞	Dog 狗	Pig 豬
1932, 1944, 1956, 1968, 1980, 1992, 2004	1933, 1945, 1957, 1969, 1981, 1993, 2005	1934, 1946, 1958, 1970, 1982, 1994, 2006	1935, 1947, 1959, 1971, 1983, 1995, 2007

Fortunes of the 12 Animals

The Tiger

1926, 1938, 1950, 1962, 1974, 1986, 1998, 2010

Note: The New Year begins February 4th

Change is the theme of 2010 for the Tiger. There are strong indications of a role change in the Tiger's current work or through a new position. The first six months of 2010 are best for making a change in employment or branching out into self-employment. Be prepared to welcome these changes without clinging to what used to be. Personal relationships will follow an uneven but generally improving course throughout the year. Money prospects are average. Tigers born in 1962 and 1974: please remember that this is a change-prone year; profits come and go easily for those doing business. There are signs of hidden backstabbers so be careful of betrayal by friends or your own staff. Try to be humble at all time to avoid nasty situations. Health-wise, it is easy to get hurt by sharp metal objects. Young Tigers and teenagers should stay away from dangerous places to avoid injury. In romance, your love life is full of changes. The Tiger will be quite emotional, easily fighting with a loved one over trivial matters. Married Tigers have a lot of quarrels this year, so take care and control your temper if you don't want the relationship to break up.

Your Benefactor is: Sheep
(1919, 1931, 1943, 1955, 1967, 1979, 1991, 2003)

12 Month Outlook For The Tiger

Solar Month	Comments
1st Month Feb 4th - Mar 5th	Normal luck. An auspicious time for you to learn or plan something for the future.
2nd Month Mar 6th - Apr 4th	Work for your goal and it will turn out quite well.
3rd Month Apr 5th - May 4th	Average luck. Advice from friends cannot be taken at face value. Your usual good judgment is at a low.
4th Month May 5th - June 5th	Good luck is predicted in money matters! Substantial gains can be expected.
5th Month June 6th - July 6th	Not a beneficial time for going out late at midnight. Be cautious of robbery.
6th Month July 7th - Aug 6th	Expenses for the month are uncertain. Do not be a guarantor. Trust nobody.
7th Month Aug 7th - Sept 7th	Keep on high alert. This is a month of conflict and tension. Take a back seat and relax.
8th Month Sept 8th - Oct 7th	Auspicious luck. Things are to your satisfaction.
9th Month Oct 8th - Nov 6th	There are small gains and big losses. Any new plan for the future requires care and consideration.
10th Month Nov 7th - Dec 6th	Busy month. Stress and tension could be higher than usual.
11th Month Dec 7th - Jan 5th	Focus on your health to prevent illness. Avoid working too much. Relax more.
12th Month Jan 6th - Feb 3rd	There is a sign of conflict. Watch out for backstabbers. Silence is golden.

The Rabbit

1927, 1939, 1951, 1963, 1975, 1987, 1999

Note: The New Year begins February 4ᵗʰ

The Tiger year holds different fortunes for males and females born in the year of the Rabbit. Males have auspicious luck while the females do not. Generally speaking, it is a good year for males to take an active stance, for example going far away from your birth place to work or study. This will help advance your future career. For female Tigers, playing safe in Tiger year is the best policy because your money luck is weak and there is a sign of financial loss. Stay away from financial speculation and avoid excessive spending. Career luck is inconsistent; obstacles stand in the way. Complications arise in the things you do, or others may sabotage your efforts. Therefore, think carefully before investing in anything. Profits come and go easily for those doing business but it is advisable to stay away from gambling. The Rabbit will generally have good health this year. Avoid stress brought on by working too much and watch out for food-related illnesses. Where romance is concerned, it will be a year of hits for male Rabbits and misses for females. Female Rabbits who are married should spend more time with their spouses to prevent a third party intruder. Moreover, an outside negative peach blossom may show up in the summer for Rabbits born in 1963.

Your Benefactor is: Monkey
(1920, 1932, 1944, 1956, 1968, 1980, 1992, 2004)

12 Month Outlook For The Rabbit

Solar Month	Comments
1st Month Feb 4th - Mar 5th	Luck goes smoothly in most everything.
2nd Month Mar 6th - Apr 4th	Things are good for male Rabbits but not for female Rabbits.
3rd Month Apr 5th - May 4th	Be patient and avoid becoming too emotional. Don't expect too much this month.
4th Month May 5th - June 5th	A month of gossip. It is easy to get a traffic ticket or a similar minor problem. A benefactor may come to you.
5th Month June 6th - July 6th	A mixture of good and bad. There are signs of sickness. Take extra care of elders within the family.
6th Month July 7th - Aug 6th	Expenses for the month are uncertain. Do not be a guarantor. Trust nobody.
7th Month Aug 7th - Sept 7th	Be wary of a trusted friend turning against you. Salaried workers may face a lot of pressure or feel frustrated.
8th Month Sept 8th - Oct 7th	Money luck sails smoothly. Things are good on average and life is quite busy. Beneficial for a long journey.
9th Month Oct 8th - Nov 6th	
10th Month Nov 7th - Dec 6th	You encounter competition, pressure, and tense relationships with people around you.
11th Month Dec 7th - Jan 5th	Average luck. There are some discomforts but nothing serious.
12th Month Jan 6th - Feb 3rd	Luck is bumpy. When you gain, watch out for possible loss.

The Dragon

1928, 1940, 1952, 1964, 1976, 1988, 2000

Note: The New Year begins February 4th

Generally speaking, this is a mixed year for the Dragon, alternating between auspicious and inauspicious. In career, you should put in more time and hard work; obstacles in the beginning can be overcome and will ultimately benefit you. However, in business dealings, it is easy to get tangled up. Pay more attention to relationships with people. Female Dragons are quite busy both physically and mentally. In the summertime, tact and tolerance are needed to avoid friction with a co-worker or someone close to you. With the Golden Cabinet shining above, money luck is average to good. However, some unexpected consuming cannot be avoided. Be on guard to prevent financial mishaps. In health, common complaints this year are insomnia, mental stress, and poor digestion. Observe good eating habits. Where romance is concerned, the Dragon's relationship with a loved one alternates between good and bad. The good news is that relationships progress faster than expected, or even march forward to the wedding chapel. The bad news is that disputes with your love will occur frequently. This is especially true with married Dragons born in 1964 and 1976. Be more communicative with your partner. He or she needs your care and understanding.

Your Benefactor is: Horse
(1930, 1942, 1954, 1966, 1978, 1990, 2002)

14

12 Month Outlook For The Dragon

Solar Month	Comments
1st Month Feb 4th - Mar 5th	Luck is average. Your plans and efforts will be rewarded in future.
2nd Month Mar 6th - Apr 4th	Tense relationships with friends or family.
3rd Month Apr 5th - May 4th	Luck is steady and climbing up; all things come out well. It is a good time to think about something new.
4th Month May 5th - June 5th	Luck is going up. This is a rewarding month!
5th Month June 6th - July 6th	Expenses for the month are uncertain. Advice from a friend cannot be taken at face value. Your usual good judgment is at low ebb.
6th Month July 7th - Aug 6th	Good opportunities come your way. Daily activities and surroundings are easier to handle than usual.
7th Month Aug 7th - Sept 7th	You may frequently feel unwell or moody.
8th Month Sept 8th - Oct 7th	Steady and smooth sailing. Good news can be expected within the family.
9th Month Oct 8th - Nov 6th	There are small gains and big losses. Any new plan for the future requires care and consideration.
10th Month Nov 7th - Dec 6th	Relaxation is the top priority this month. Be careful of illness.
11th Month Dec 7th - Jan 5th	Be careful of sharp objects that can cause bleeding.
12th Month Jan 6th - Feb 3rd	Strong and enjoyable Peach Blossom. Love partnerships are strengthened. Your mate or date knows just how to keep you smiling.

The Snake

Note: The New Year begins February 4th

The female Snake has better luck because the Tai Yin Star is shining above. This brings good money-making opportunities for the self-employed. This is a year to start any one of your plans to achieve long-term goals and lay a firm foundation for the future. Salaried workers look forward to a promotion or ask for a pay raise. A special opportunity exists if you are willing to commute a longer distance to your work. The male Snake does not have the same luck as the female in the Tiger year. Give full attention to whatever you are working on. Think before saying or doing anything that you know is not quite in accordance with rules and regulations. Refuse to rise to a challenge even if you believe you can win. If you control your temper and sugarcoat your words, you should get all the cooperation you need. Health-wise, apart from insomnia and ear or blood-related problems, the Snake will be relatively healthy in the Tiger year. Where romance is concerned, males may experience mood swings. For females, romantic encounters are abundant, but cannot last long; though you have a likeable personality, conditions are too quiet to expect responses. Married couples can be quite emotional and lose control. Be more communicative with your partner to avoid misunderstandings.

Your Benefactor is: Tiger
(1920, 1932, 1944, 1956, 1968, 1980, 1992, 2004)

12 Month Outlook For The Snake

Solar Month	Comments
1st Month Feb 4th - Mar 5th	Luck is noticeably moving upward for females, but this month males pay more and receive less.
2nd Month Mar 6th - Apr 4th	A stable month for everything.
3rd Month Apr 5th - May 4th	Average luck. Be extra careful of money loss and unexpected expenses.
4th Month May 5th - June 5th	Money luck alternates between good and bad. Expenses for the month are uncertain.
5th Month June 6th - July 6th	Good for traveling and going abroad: you may receive unexpected benefits.
6th Month July 7th - Aug 6th	Do not be a guarantor. Trust nobody.
7th Month Aug 7th - Sept 7th	Life is average for females. Males can easily lose money because of a flirtation or romance.
8th Month Sept 8th - Oct 7th	A month of gain and loss; easy come and easy go. Don't expect a lot.
9th Month Oct 8th - Nov 6th	Money and career luck are in good sight.
10th Month Nov 7th - Dec 6th	An underlying danger awaits you this month. Be careful of injuries and cuts.
11th Month Dec 7th - Jan 5th	A Peach Blossom star and other auspicious stars are shining above! Everything is joyous.
12th Month Jan 6th - Feb 3rd	Life is good and things are going well. A good time to develop something new in your life.

The Horse

1918, 1930, 1942, 1954, 1966, 1978, 1990, 2002

Note: The New Year begins February 4th

This year the Horse encounters obstacles in career and confusion in love. This is an unstable year, a time of floating and sinking. Where career is concerned, your gains will not be proportional to the effort you put in. Be patient and tolerant. Take baby steps as there is no big leap this year. However, if you persist in taking the initiative and are decisive, you can make the Tiger year gainful. A number of obstacles and setbacks await you in spring. However, luck will improve in the second half of the year. This is a good time to learn something new. Reserve your energy and be well-prepared for a more auspicious time when better opportunities will come. With money, do not have too many lofty dreams or take short-cuts with risky investments. Side-income prospects are good for the Horses born in 1954 or 1978. Health-wise, watch out for eye diseases, heart related problems, and burns. Young Horses and teenagers must stay away from fire and things like firecrackers or guns. The path to romance is not going to be smooth but is full of hiccoughs for singles. Do not expect too much from relationships. You will only be asking trouble if you ignore the unfavorable time factor, persist in being willful, and follow your passion too much. There is danger that married Horses born in 1966 or 1978 will get involved in a scandalous affair.

Your Benefactor is: Dragon
(1928, 1940, 1952, 1964, 1976, 1988, 2000)

12 Month Outlook For The Horse

Solar Month	Comments
1st Month Feb 4th - Mar 5th	In these two months, backstabbers are around - you need to watch out when dealing with people. Be cautious with your health to avoid an illness which may visit you or an elderly family member.
2nd Month Mar 6th - Apr 4th	
3rd Month Apr 5th - May 4th	Put aside all thoughts of work responsibilities. Relaxation is the top priority.
4th Month May 5th - June 5th	Life is good and things are going well. You may meet someone you fancy and experience mood swings.
5th Month June 6th - July 6th	Tense relationships with friends or family. Avoid becoming too emotional.
6th Month July 7th - Aug 6th	Gossip tangles things up.
7th Month Aug 7th - Sept 7th	A very auspicious time, big gains, small losses. Things are smooth.
8th Month Sept 8th - Oct 7th	This is a rewarding month! Your goals can easily be achieved. Married Horses should be wary of sex traps.
9th Month Oct 8th - Nov 6th	A good time for traveling. Lots of confusion in dealing with things.
10th Month Nov 7th - Dec 6th	Money luck strongly moves upward.
11th Month Dec 7th - Jan 5th	Strong Peach Blossom (romance, social relationships). A helpful benefactor shows up and offers assistance.
12th Month Jan 6th - Feb 3rd	Be conservative and do things with double caution to end a year that has been full of obscurities and hurdles.

19

The Sheep

1931, 1943, 1955, 1967, 1979, 1991, 2003

Note: The New Year begins February 4th

Two major auspicious stars shining above will bring wealth and fame for the Sheep in 2010. Career and money prospects are most promising. You may want to consider venturing abroad or pushing ahead with personal plans. Luck is smooth for everything you plan. Most projects hit the target. Money luck is strong, with big gains and small losses. Seize this opportunity to take a big step forward and build your lifetime foundation. With extra strong luck, you receive double benefits for the work exerted. Career and money luck are at their best in beginning of the year: spring and early summer. However, there is strong pressure from the competition for the self-employed. Salaried workers may discover a new source of income, and there is a sign of conflict with colleagues. There is a Chinese saying: "Harmony breeds prosperity." Therefore, the best policy is to be humble at all times and try to maintain a cordial relationship with people around you. In health, there are no signs of major problems. However, take precaution against allergies and the flu. Romance will be fruitful this year. For those who are single, love is rosy and there is great opportunity for marriage. For married Sheep, there is a tendency to get involved in a short term romance.

Your Benefactor is: Dog
(1922, 1934, 1946, 1958, 1970, 1982, 1994, 2006)

12 Month Outlook For The Sheep

Solar Month	Comments
1st Month Feb 4th - Mar 5th	Good time to develop something new. Salaried workers can expect a promotion.
2nd Month Mar 6th - Apr 4th **3rd Month** Apr 5th - May 4th	Luck is smooth for everything you plan. Most projects will hit the target. Career and money prospects are rewarding. The harder you work, the more you gain.
4th Month May 5th - June 5th	Life is enjoyable.
5th Month June 6th - July 6th	Luck is unstable. Money luck is up and down. Risky investments and business deals are not to be taken at face value.
6th Month July 7th - Aug 6th	Things emerge well. Strong Peach Blossom!
7th Month Aug 7th - Sept 7th	Good opportunities come your way. Be careful of your speech to avoid misunderstandings.
8th Month Sept 8th - Oct 7th	Things are steadily going up. A good month to receive a marriage proposal!
9th Month Oct 8th - Nov 6th	Take care of your health, and watch out for the flu and insomnia.
10th Month Nov 7th - Dec 6th	Turn down all invitations. Spending has to be cut back to necessities only.
11th Month Dec 7th - Jan 5th	Things are busy and marching forward.
12th Month Jan 6th - Feb 3rd	Strong good luck so put more of yourself into everything that you do. The gains are bountiful.

The Monkey

1920, 1932, 1944, 1956, 1968, 1980, 1992, 2004

Note: The New Year begins February 4th

This is the Po Sui or year breaker for the Monkey. Change plays a major part in every aspect of your career this year. Carefully find the jade among the trash and pay close attention to golden opportunities that other people are likely to overlook. Conflict with others will arise frequently. Sugarcoat your words and use soft tactics when dealing with difficult situations. In career, success and failure both come easily. Give full attention to whatever you are working on this year. If someone's decision is going to affect your options, keep your cool in whatever you do. Do not trust anyone blindly lest you get cheated. Be especially cautious about signing documents. Read all the fine print first and be sure you understand what it means. Due to the Big Consumer Star shining above, money goes out easily, so be prepared for the worst. There is a need to budget wisely. Avoid financial speculation. Health is average; the physical discomfort you feel is caused by your moodiness. You may require a doctor visit for your lungs and chest. Those born in 1944 may have to undergo surgery. In romance, the Monkey will be quite emotional and easily fight with a loved one over trivial matters. This may lead to separation. The best way to avoid this is to be patient and do not nitpick or argue.

Your Benefactor is: Ox
(1925, 1937, 1949, 1961, 1973, 1985, 1997, 2009)

12 Month Outlook For The Monkey

Solar Month	Comments
1st Month Feb 4th - Mar 5th	Some obstacles lie ahead, so this is not the time to plan something new. Prevent unnecessary spending.
2nd Month Mar 6th - Apr 4th	Career and money prospects are in good sight. You may encounter minor conflicts.
3rd Month Apr 5th - May 4th	Things are average. Be careful: a minor illness may visit you.
4th Month May 5th - June 5th	Lots of confusion in dealing with things. There are a number of squabbles. Be on your guard.
5th Month June 6th - July 6th	Stay on high alert - something good could turn into something bad.
6th Month July 7th - Aug 6th	Mixed good and bad. Double-check all work, especially that done by others on your behalf.
7th Month Aug 7th - Sept 7th	There are signs of a setback in career and money matters. There is a need to budget wisely.
8th Month Sept 8th - Oct 7th	Beneficial for venturing overseas.
9th Month Oct 8th - Nov 6th	This is a great time to push ahead with your personal plans or expand your business and pursue your goals.
10th Month Nov 7th - Dec 6th	Luck is moving upward. Life is quite busy with social activities.
11th Month Dec 7th - Jan 5th	There are small gains and big losses. Be careful to avoid cuts, burns and the flu.
12th Month Jan 6th - Feb 3rd	Watch out for an illness. Get enough rest. There is a disturbance in love or a conflict in another relationship.

The Rooster

1921, 1933, 1945, 1957, 1969, 1981, 1993, 2005

Note: The New Year begins February 4th

Roosters will find the Tiger year a blessed one. This is a highly rewarding year. Career and money prospects are in your favor. Bosses think highly of their Rooster salaried workers. If you are thinking of changing jobs or striking out on your own, this is the time to do it. The self-employed can expand their business; it is a good time for new ventures. There are lots of opportunities waiting at the front door but stiff competition lies ahead. However, Roosters can easily become stressed out and moody, so plenty of rest is recommended. Career and money luck alternate between good and bad during spring and summer. Watch out for financial losses. Health-wise, common complaints this year are problems of the digestive system, constipation, and insomnia. Romance is fruitful and it sparkles! This is a good year for the single Rooster to get married, but avoid ruining a perfect relationship in a moment of willfulness. This is also an easy year for female Roosters to get pregnant. Due to quite strong Peach Blossom for both male and the female Roosters in the Tiger year, married Roosters should not try to pick those wild blossoms from the roadside or you will find them difficult to get rid of, bringing you headaches.

Your Benefactor is: Rat
(1924, 1936, 1948, 1960, 1972, 1984, 1996, 2008)

12 Month Outlook For The Rooster

Solar Month	Comments
1st Month Feb 4th - Mar 5th	Lots of social opportunities: good gains and good Peach Blossom.
2nd Month Mar 6th - Apr 4th	Money and career luck is smooth. This is a good time to start a new project or learn something new.
3rd Month Apr 5th - May 4th	An auspicious star is shining above! An unexpected good surprise will come.
4th Month May 5th - June 5th	Take care of your health. Stay away from the sick if you do not want to stricken by illness.
5th Month June 6th - July 6th	Life is busy. Stress is higher than usual.
6th Month July 7th - Aug 6th	Average luck. Not too many obstacles, nor too much excitement.
7th Month Aug 7th - Sept 7th	For males, career and love are both happy, but these are frustrating for females.
8th Month Sept 8th - Oct 7th	This is a rewarding month! Your goals can easily be achieved.
9th Month Oct 8th - Nov 6th	Auspicious luck: Love and career go smoothly.
10th Month Nov 7th - Dec 6th	Be ready to take advantage of a change this month. Good opportunity.
11th Month Dec 7th - Jan 5th	Big losses, small gains. Watch your speech. Don't be aggressive.
12th Month Jan 6th - Feb 3rd	Money luck is strong. You may receive some unexpected benefit.

The Dog

1922, 1934, 1946, 1958, 1970, 1982, 1994, 2006

Note: The New Year begins February 4ᵗʰ

 This is a challenging year. Luck is unstable. It appears like a good year, but there is bad hidden in the good. There are signs of conflict in career and lots of confusion in dealing with things. Sudden changes may throw your life into disarray. This is not a good time to expand or switch careers as you may end up being worse off than ever. You need to be very careful if you plan to make investments. However, this is a beneficial year for Dog writers, actors, and individuals who work in entertainment industry. Students can expect good academic results. It is a good idea to venture abroad after the summer; there are prospects for overseas ventures for working people, and good academic results for those still in school. Again, care is needed; there is a sign of being cheated. With many temptations to spend money, the year calls for careful financial management and restraint. Though you may occasionally suffer from stress or moodiness, you are generally in good health. Keep an eye on the young and old in the family. They may have an accident or fall ill. Romance is not going to be smooth sailing this year, so it is natural for you to feel empty and lonely. Disputes with your loved one will occur frequently. This is especially true for married couples.

Your Benefactor is: Pig
(1923, 1935, 1947, 1959, 1971, 1983, 1995, 2007)

12 Month Outlook For The Dog

Solar Month	Comments
1st Month Feb 4th - Mar 5th	Be cautious; family members could have health problems. Avoid visiting hospitals.
2nd Month Mar 6th - Apr 4th	Auspicious stars shine above! Fight hard for what you want and you will get it.
3rd Month Apr 5th - May 4th	Caution is the keyword of the month. What you are thinking may be the opposite of what it is.
4th Month May 5th - June 5th	Conditions are easygoing and comfortable.
5th Month June 6th - July 6th	Upsets may crop up when you least expect them. A project that has been moving under a full head of steam may suddenly grind to halt.
6th Month July 7th - Aug 6th	Your life is going on an even keel!
7th Month Aug 7th - Sept 7th	Traveling to other places will bring you some unexpected benefits.
8th Month Sept 8th - Oct 7th	Luck is average. Be careful about over-spending.
9th Month Oct 8th - Nov 6th	Check every document carefully before you sign it. Trust no one.
10th Month Nov 7th - Dec 6th	Money luck is strong. An auspicious time for you to do business abroad or with foreign companies.
11th Month Dec 7th - Jan 5th	Good opportunities for promotion. Career and money prospects are rewarding.
12th Month Jan 6th - Feb 3rd	There might be conflicts with others. Be humble, as excessive self-esteem will lead to negative results.

The Pig

1923, 1935, 1947, 1959, 1971, 1983, 1995, 2007

Note: The New Year begins February 4th

Since hidden danger lurks for the Pig in the Tiger year, things may go quite wrong. Because there is a sign of getting hit by lawsuits, you cannot afford to be careless when dealing with people or signing contracts. Where career is concerned, your gains will not be proportional to the great effort you put in. Be careful of financial losses due to carelessness in middle of the year. Cast away any thoughts of greed to avoid financial mishap. Be on guard in whatever you do during the summer and do not leave anything to luck. Refrain from gambling and alcohol. But don't be depressed; if you persist in taking the initiative, are decisive, and put double the effort into your work, you can make 2010 a gainful year. A big unexpected gift will come the way of Pigs born in 1983. Health-wise, this is quite an unstable year. Minor illness visits you non-stop; injuries to your limbs may result from accidents. Those born in 1947 and 1959 should refrain from visiting the sick. Where romance is concerned, your love life is full of setbacks. Though Pigs may date quite a lot, it is difficult to differentiate a sincere relationship from one that is not. Married couples will blow hot and cold and quarrels are easily aroused.

Your Benefactor is: Rooster
(1933, 1945, 1957, 1969, 1981, 1993, 2005)

12 Month Outlook For The Pig

Solar Month	Comments
1st Month Feb 4th - Mar 5th	Though there is pressure on your job, money and career are in good sight.
2nd Month Mar 6th - Apr 4th	Strong Peach Blossom energy is around. You feel great. Your work is mostly rewarded.
3rd Month Apr 5th - May 4th	Be tolerant. You are prone to get angry over the most trivial matters.
4th Month May 5th - June 5th	Trust nobody! It is easy to have a loss.
5th Month June 6th - July 6th	Luck is mixed between good and bad. Keep alert and do not take any risk if you are doubtful.
6th Month July 7th - Aug 6th	This is an enjoyable month for females, but a dangerous month for males in a love relationship.
7th Month Aug 7th - Sept 7th	There is a hint of anger or despair. Keep your emotions under tight control in all situations to avoid conflicts.
8th Month Sept 8th - Oct 7th	Luck is unstable. You may encounter conflicts.
9th Month Oct 8th - Nov 6th	Be conservative. Avoid being hasty or greedy so as to prevent financial mishaps.
10th Month Nov 7th - Dec 6th	Things will go mostly as you wish. Whether working for a boss or for yourself, results are determined by your own extra effort.
11th Month Dec 7th - Jan 5th	There are signs that family disharmony can occur.
12th Month Jan 6th - Feb 3rd	Beware of gossip and backstabbing. Do what you usually do. Say less.

The Rat

1924, 1936, 1948, 1960, 1972, 1984, 1996, 2008

Note: The New Year begins February 4th

The Tiger year promises to be a fruitful one for Rats. It is generally indicated that financial interests are accented at this time. This year's communications should include a few that make you very happy. They may concern anything from a much desired social invitation, a glamorous travel opportunity, good news concerning a business deal or wage increase, and/or celebrating the news of a marriage or baby. Strong money luck and substantial gains can be expected by taking a long journey between August 7 and September 6. However the period from September 7 through October 15 holds signs of financial mishap. You are likely to incur unnecessary expenditures. There is a need to budget wisely and keep expenses under control. Be conservative and on guard in career or job changes. It is not an appropriate time to make such changes. Hold your ground unless convinced that changes are necessary. Health-wise, common complaints for the Rat are insomnia and stress brought on by working too much. Those born in 1936 should stay away from places such as hospitals where contagious diseases can be found. Romance is fruitful because of the Sui He star. There is a great opportunity for marriage. Married Rat relationships will be relatively harmonious through the year.

Your Benefactor is: Rabbit
(1927, 1939, 1951, 1963, 1975, 1987, 1999)

12 Month Outlook For The Rat	
Solar Month	**Comments**
1st Month Feb 4th - Mar 5th	Luck is still good and smooth. This is a good time for developing something new.
2nd Month Mar 6th - Apr 4th	Be careful of being attacked by sudden illness.
3rd Month Apr 5th - May 4th	This is an auspicious month. Cooperation with others will enable you to receive great benefits.
4th Month May 5th - June 5th	This is a rewarding month for both romance and business. It is also a good time to discuss marriage plans.
5th Month June 6th - July 6th	Things are steadily going up.
6th Month July 7th - Aug 6th	Refuse to be rushed into a decision that will have far-reaching effects.
7th Month Aug 7th - Sept 7th	There are benefits for venturing overseas.
8th Month Sept 8th - Oct 7th	Be alert for signs of overspending or money loss.
9th Month Oct 8th - Nov 6th	Be conservative and on guard in career or job changes.
10th Month Nov 7th - Dec 6th	A good opportunity is awaiting you and there is something good to celebrate!
11th Month Dec 7th - Jan 5th	Don't be aggressive. Regarding money, trust no one.
12th Month Jan 6th - Feb 3rd	Good timing! You will be in the right place at the right time

The Ox

1925, 1937, 1949, 1961, 1973, 1985, 1997, 2009

Note: The New Year begins February 4ᵗʰ

This is a year to be conservative and not to be aggressive when embarking on a new career for the self-employed. It is a year of pressure for the Ox. Be forewarned of some obstacles you may encounter. You are prone to temper outbursts and tend to get angry over the most trivial matters. Especially in June, try not to get involved in matters that do not concern you to prevent trouble and losses. Yet, salaried workers will gain recognition at the workplace which will lead to promotion in turn. Therefore, you should consider attending self-improvement or job-related courses. Money prospects alternate between good and bad. Investments should be made only after careful consideration. Learn to spend your money wisely and avoid financial speculation. Health-wise, though you may occasionally suffer from allergies or insomnia, you are generally in good health this year. The Ox born in 1949 or 1997 is quite accident-prone during the summer. To prevent accidents and injuries, stay away from strenuous sports and avoid scaling heights. Where romance is concerned, a fruitful relationship will come the way of the single Ox. This is a good year for courting couples to get married. Those who are married should do something to prevent your partner from straying.

Your Benefactor is: Snake
(1929, 1941, 1953, 1965, 1977, 1989, 2001)

12 Month Outlook For The Ox	
Solar Month	**Comments**
1st Month Feb 4th - Mar 5th	This is a rewarding month for both romance and social relationships.
2nd Month Mar 6th - Apr 4th	You may frequently feel unwell or moody.
3rd Month Apr 5th - May 4th	Money prospects are at their best for males. Life is average for females.
4th Month May 5th - June 5th	Be alert for signs of overspending or backstabbers.
5th Month June 6th - July 6th	All things are relatively peaceful.
6th Month July 7th - Aug 6th	To prevent accidents and injuries, stay away from strenuous sports and avoid scaling heights.
7th Month Aug 7th - Sept 7th	This month holds good fortune for proceeding with something new or expanding your career.
8th Month Sept 8th - Oct 7th	Exceptionally good for venturing overseas.
9th Month Oct 8th - Nov 6th	Beware of falling into a trap. For males, stay away from alcohol and sex.
10th Month Nov 7th - Dec 6th	Luck is low. To be safe, pay more attention to your health and do not visit sick people.
11th Month Dec 7th - Jan 5th	Normal luck. Relaxation is the top priority.
12th Month Jan 6th - Feb 3rd	There are signs of unexpected gains and a benefactor is coming forward.

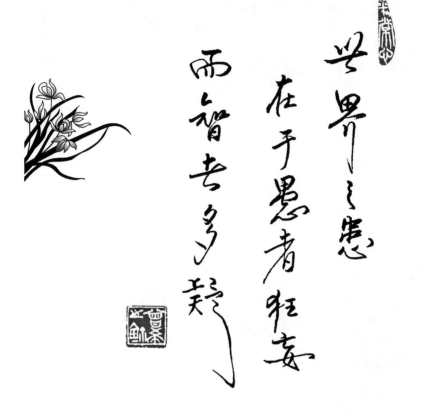

世界之患
在于愚者狂妄
而智者多疑

The trouble with the world is that,
the stupid are cocksure and
the intelligent are full of doubt

Calligraphy by Larry Sang

Li Ming

TABLE 1 立 命 LI MING (establish fate): STEP 1: DETERMINE YOUR PALACE 立 命 LI MING for 2010

This is another system for making annual predictions:

★ First, use Table 1, based on your month and time of birth.

★ Take the results of Table 1, and use them in Table 2, along with your year of birth, to find the palace of Li Ming for 2010.

★ Once you know the palace of Li Ming, read the prediction that follows for that palace.

		Born After:											
Birth Hour:		Jan 21 1st Month	Feb 19 2nd Month	Mar 20 3rd Month	Apr 20 4th Month	May 21 5th Month	Jun 21 6th Month	Jul 23 7th Month	Aug 23 8th Month	Sep 23 9th Month	Oct 23 10th Month	Nov 22 11th Month	Dec 22 12th Month
Zi	11pm-1am	Mao	Yin	Chou	Zi	Hai	Xu	You	Shen	Wei	Wu	Si	Chen
Chou	1-3am	Yin	Chou	Zi	Hai	Xu	You	Shen	Wei	Wu	Si	Chen	Mao
Yin	3-5am	Chou	Zi	Hai	Xu	You	Shen	Wei	Wu	Si	Chen	Mao	Yin
Mao	5-7am	Zi	Hai	Xu	You	Shen	Wei	Wu	Si	Chen	Mao	Yin	Chou
Chen	7-9am	Hai	Xu	You	Shen	Wei	Wu	Si	Chen	Mao	Yin	Chou	Zi
Si	9-11am	Xu	You	Shen	Wei	Wu	Si	Chen	Mao	Yin	Chou	Zi	Hai
Wu	11am-1pm	You	Shen	Wei	Wu	Si	Chen	Mao	Yin	Chou	Zi	Hai	Xu
Wei	1-3pm	Shen	Wei	Wu	Si	Chen	Mao	Yin	Chou	Zi	Hai	Xu	You
Shen	3-5pm	Wei	Wu	Si	Chen	Mao	Yin	Chou	Zi	Hai	Xu	You	Shen
You	5-7pm	Wu	Si	Chen	Mao	Yin	Chou	Zi	Hai	Xu	You	Shen	Wei
Xu	7-9pm	Si	Chen	Mao	Yin	Chou	Zi	Hai	Xu	You	Shen	Wei	Wu
Hai	9-11pm	Che	Mao	Yin	Chou	Zi	Hai	Xu	You	Shen	Wei	Wu	Si

Notes:

These months are different from the solar (Feng Shui/Four Pillars) months, and also are different from the lunar months. They begin on the *Qi* of the *Twenty-Four Solar Jieqi*. If born within a day of these month dates, please consult a *Ten-Thousand Year Calendar* to determine exactly which is your birth month in this system. It is not necessary for you to understand the Chinese terms in the tables. Just follow the tables to the correct palace for you.

TABLE 2 — LI MING (establish fate): STEP 2: PALACE FOR A YIN (TIGER) YEAR — LI MING for 2010

Li Ming:	Birth Year:											
	Rat Zi	Ox Chou	Tiger Yin	Rabbit Mao	Dragon Chen	Snake Si	Horse Wu	Sheep Wei	Monkey Shen	Rooster You	Dog Xu	Pig Hai
Zi	Xu	Hai	Zi	Chou	Yin	Mao	Chen	Si	Wu	Wei	Shen	You
Chou	Hai	Zi	Chou	Yin	Mao	Chen	Si	Wu	Wei	Shen	You	Xu
Yin	Zi	Chou	Yin	Mao	Chen	Si	Wu	Wei	Shen	You	Xu	Hai
Mao	Chou	Yin	Mao	Chen	Si	Wu	Wei	Shen	You	Xu	Hai	Zi
Chen	Yin	Mao	Chen	Si	Wu	Wei	Shen	You	Xu	Hai	Zi	Chou
Si	Mao	Chen	Si	Wu	Wei	Shen	You	Xu	Hai	Zi	Chou	Yin
Wu	Chen	Si	Wu	Wei	Shen	You	Xu	Hai	Zi	Chou	Yin	Mao
Wei	Si	Wu	Wei	Shen	You	Xu	Hai	Zi	Chou	Yin	Mao	Chen
Shen	Wu	Wei	Shen	You	Xu	Hai	Zi	Chou	Yin	Mao	Chen	Si
You	Wei	Shen	You	Xu	Hai	Zi	Chou	Yin	Mao	Chen	Si	Wu
Xu	Shen	You	Xu	Hai	Zi	Chou	Yin	Mao	Chen	Si	Wu	Wei
Hai	You	Xu	Hai	Zi	Chou	Yin	Mao	Chen	Si	Wu	Wei	Shen

Notes:

✩ Take the Palace of Li Ming, found in Table 1, and compare it to the year of birth to find the palace for 2010, a Yin (Tiger) year.

✩ Use January 21st as the beginning of the new year for finding the birth year. If the date falls within one day of January 21st, check in a *Ten-Thousand Year Calendar* to be sure. If the birth date is between January 1st and January 20th, consider the person as belonging to the previous year in this system.

✩ The predictions described below go from January 20th, 2010 until January 19th, 2011.

37

Li Ming Palace Reading

Z i

The Tai Sui star, together with two auspicious stars, makes this a year full of positive changes. A profitable investment opportunity awaits the self-employed. A promotion and pay raise will come the way of salaried workers. Make full use of the year by working hard and fighting for what you want. Be careful of overspending. There are signs of financial mishap when traveling long distances.

Chou

Li Ming here is good in all four seasons. Tai Yang, together with other auspicious stars, is shining above. Take hold of this good luck to achieve your goals. Your source of money moves upwards. A benefactor of the opposite sex will show up for females, while a benefactor of same sex will show up for males. Regarding a change of jobs, early spring and late summer are the best time to do it.

Y i n

Be patient and do not get discouraged easily. It is not a year to expand or to be overly optimistic. Whatever is accomplished requires double effort to receive a single gain. Indulgence brings unexpected consumption of small things. Yi Ma star shines above, so there are good money opportunities if you go far from your current working place. There are signs of job changes or moving your house.

Mao

The four seasons pass by happily. With Hong Luan star shining above, singles will easily find a suitable life partner. There is a sign of marriage. Any relationship that is in the budding stage can move ahead if you are willing to be more aggressive. Females enjoy better money luck and their careers will go more smoothly than for males. Be cautious of your speech. There are signs of conflict in relationships.

Chen
If Li Ming is here, this is an excellent time to embark into higher education or learning something new. Students can expect good academic results. 2010 will seem unusually long to you because of your moodiness. You can advance rapidly in your career or move up socially if you are willing to make an effort. Observe good eating habits and watch out for sprains and fractures.

Si
It is significant that the Lu Can star is together with Yue De. If Li Ming is here, you can make use of this strong money qi to help you reach a financial goal. However, there may be a slight change in your fiscal position because of the presence of an inauspicious star named Xiao Hao, but nothing to fret about. Avoid overworking. You may get sick, if you over-extend yourself.

Wu
This year Sui Po is in Ming Palace and Tai Sui is opposite, so it will be a year of breakthrough or change. Conflict with others will arise easily. Not a year to expand or be overly optimistic. Things beyond your control suddenly change. With an inauspicious Da Hao star, it is a sign of unnecessary increases in expenditures. Watch out for cash-flow problems and budget wisely. It is unfavorable for legal affairs.

Wei
Two auspicious stars, Zi Wei and Long De, shine above giving you energy and enthusiasm. You will be busy, ambitious and assertive, willing to fight for what you want. Your wit will come in handy. Though this is a relatively good year, care must be taken to prevent acts of sabotage by others due to jealousy. The best policy is to be humble at all time to prevent nasty situations.

Shen If Li Ming is here, you will encounter backstabbers and find it easy to arouse misunderstandings between you and your working partners and friends. Be alert for signs of backstabbing. Do not trust anyone blindly lest you be cheated. Don't hold high expectations about money beyond your ability. However, there is benefit for writers or people in the entertainment industries.

You The year begins with a fortunate trine linking Tian Xi, Tian De and Fu Xing. Dreams can come true regarding financial or love matters. Be prudent and realistic, and work hard to accomplish your goals. It is going to be a beautiful year for romance. Those who are married should avoid getting involved in extramarital affairs.

Xu Inauspicious stars gather together. It is appropriate to be cautious and prudent in all matters. This year is not a time to be speculative. Be careful of injury to any of the four limbs by sharp metal objects. However, the presence of the Jie Shen star will finally bring resolution when unhappy matters occur. Take care of elderly family members. Avoid visiting hospitals or attending funerals.

Hai All four seasons bring peace and prosperity. Both males and females increase their blessings. Travel puts you in contact with someone who benefits your career in the future. You may suffer financial losses through fraud. Jointly held finances require attention; this warning must be given. You may fall sick easily for no apparent reason. Injuries to four limbs may result from an accident.

Liu Ren

Liu Ren (六壬)(小六壬)

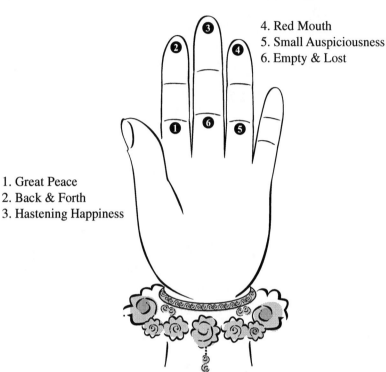

4. Red Mouth
5. Small Auspiciousness
6. Empty & Lost

1. Great Peace
2. Back & Forth
3. Hastening Happiness

CALCULATION:
When something out of the ordinary spontaneously happens,
you can determine the meaning of the omen with *Liu Ren*.
Here is the calculation:

1. Use the left hand. Start in position 1, Great Peace (大安 da an) and always move clockwise.
2. Count clockwise through the six positions for today's *lunar* month. The Great Peace position corresponds to the first lunar month. (Refer to the *Ten-Thousand Year Calendar* page at the end of this *Guide*. Find today's date, then read the month number at the top of the column.)
3. Count the position found in Step 2 as the first day of the lunar month. Count clockwise through the six positions to today, the current day of the lunar month. (Find today's date in the *Ten-Thousand Year Calendar* page, then read the day number on the side at the end of the row.)

4. Count the position found in Step 3 as the first double hour.
   Count clockwise through the six positions to the current double hour.
5. Look up the interpretation of this palace on page 44-45.

HOUR TABLE

Hour	During Standard Time	During Daylight Savings Time
1	11 pm - 1 am	midnight to 2 am
2	1 - 3 am	2 - 4 am
3	3 - 5 am	4 - 6 am
4	5 - 7 am	6 - 8 am
5	7 - 9 am	8 - 10 am
6	9 - 11 am	10 - noon
7	11 am - 1 pm	noon to 2 pm
8	1 - 3 pm	2 - 4 pm
9	3 - 5 pm	4 - 6 pm
10	5 - 7 pm	6 - 8 pm
11	7 - 9 pm	8 - 10 pm
12	9 - 11 pm	10 - midnight

Note: for 11 pm to midnight during standard time, use the next day's date. For example, if it is 11:15 pm on February 12th, then count it as February 13th.

Example: April 19th, 2010, 10:15 am.

Start in Position One.

April 19th is in the column that says third month at the top.

So we go to Position Three.

April 19th is the sixth day of the third month.

Start where we left off in Position Three and call that 1.

Count clockwise to the 6th position from there: Position Two.

Start in Position Two and count for the hour.

Whether it is Daylight Savings Time or not, 10:15 am is the 6th hour.

Count 6 positions, with Position Two as the beginning, and end up in Position One.

This is the outcome:

Position One is Great Peace.
Read the text and apply it to the situation.

INTERPRETATION

1. Great Peace (大安 da an): The person in question has not moved at this time. This position belongs to wood element and the east. Generally in planning matters, use 1, 5, and 7. This position belongs to the four limbs. Helpful people are found in the southwest. Avoid the east. Children, women, and the six domestic animals are frightened.

In Great Peace, every activity prospers. Seek wealth in the southwest. Lost items are not far away. The house is secure and peaceful. The person you expect has not left yet. Illness is not serious. Military generals return home to the fields. Look for opportunities and push your luck.

2. Back and Forth (留連 liu lian): The person you expect is not returning yet. This position belongs to water element and the north. Generally in planning matters, use 2, 8, and 10. This position belongs to the kidneys and stomach. Helpful people are found in the south. Avoid the north. Children wander the road as disembodied spirits.

With Back and Forth, activities are difficult to achieve. You have not adequately planned for your goals. Official activities are delayed. Those who have gone do not return from their journey yet. Lost items appear in the south. Hurry and ask for what you want and you will get results. But guard against gossip and disputes. Family members for the moment are so-so.

3. Hastening Happiness (速喜 su xi):The expected person arrives shortly. This position belongs to fire element and the south. Generally in planning matters, use 3, 6, and 9. This position belongs to the heart and brain. Helpful people are found in the southwest. Avoid the south. Children, women, and animals are frightened.

With Hastening Happiness, happiness arrives. Seek wealth toward the south. Lost items are found between 11 a.m. and 5 p.m. if you ask a passerby about it. Official activities have blessing and virtue. Sick people have no misfortune. Auspicious for the fields, house, and the six livestock. You receive news from someone far away.

4. Red Mouth (赤口 chi kou): An inauspicious time for official activities. This position belongs to metal element and the west. Generally in planning matters, use 4, 7, and 10. This position belongs to the lungs and stomach. Helpful people are found in the east. Avoid the west. Children are bewildered young spirits.

Red Mouth governs quarrels and disputes. Be cautious about legal matters. Quickly go search for lost items. Travelers experience a fright. The six domestic animals give you trouble. The sick should go to the west. Furthermore, you must guard against being cursed. Fear catching epidemic diseases.

5. Small Auspiciousness (小吉 xiao ji): The expected person comes in a happy time. This position belongs to wood element and all directions. Generally in planning matters, use 1, 5, and 7. This position belongs to the liver and intestines. Helpful people are found in the southwest. Avoid the east. Children, women, and the six domestic animals are frightened.

Small Auspiciousness is most auspicious and prosperous. Your road is smooth. Spirits come announcing good news. Lost items are located in the southwest. Travelers promptly arrive. Relations with others are extremely strong. Everything is harmonious. A sick person should pray to heaven.

6. Empty and Lost (空亡 kong wang): News you expect does not come at this time. This position belongs to earth element. Generally in planning matters, use 3, 6, and 9. This position belongs to the spleen and brain. Helpful people are found in the north. Watch out for the health of your children. Males feel pressure. The activities of females get no results.

Spirits are often unreasonable or perverse. Seeking wealth is without benefit. There is disaster for travelers. Lost items will not appear. Official activities bring punishment and damage. Sick people meet a dark ghost. To be secure and peaceful, get release from calamity by sacrifice and prayer.

Example: You arrive at the airport, but your friend who was supposed to pick you up is not there and does not answer his cell phone. You use Liu Ren to find out what is going on.

Today's time and date: March 25th, 2010, 8:30 am

A. Start in Position One.
B. March 25th is in the column that says second month at the top. So we go to Position Two.
   March 25th is the tenth day of the second month.
   Start where we left off in Position Two and call that 1.
C. Count clockwise to the 10th position from there: Position Five.
   Start in Position Five and count for the hour.
   It is 8:30 a.m., the 5th hour.
D. Count 5 positions, with Position Five as the beginning, and end up in Position Three.

This is the outcome:

Position Three is Hastening Happiness
Read the text and apply it to the situation. Hastening Happiness begins with "The expected person arrives shortly." You wait calmly for ten minutes and your ride arrives. He tells you traffic delayed him and he forgot his cell phone.

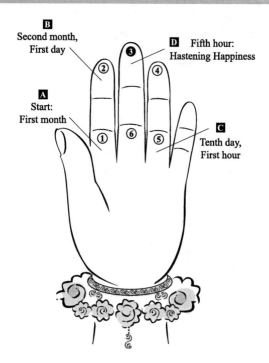

B
Second month,
First day

D Fifth hour:
Hastening Happiness

A
Start:
First month

C
Tenth day,
First hour

Omen

Omens

In Chinese almanacs, there are often listings of predictions based on omens. We include a few below. Have fun with it and don't take it too seriously.

Omens from the Twitch of an Eye		
Time	**Eye**	**This is an omen of:**
11pm-1am	left	Meeting a benefactor.
zi	right	Having a good meal.
1-3am	left	Having anxiety.
chou	right	Someone thinking about you.
3-5am	left	Someone coming from afar.
yin	right	A happy matter arriving.
5-7am	left	The coming of an important guest.
mao	right	Something peaceful, safe, and auspicious.
7-9am	left	A guest coming from afar.
chen	right	Injury or harm.
9-11am	left	Having a good meal.
si	right	Something inauspicious.
11am-1pm	left	Having a good meal.
wu	right	An inauspicious matter.
1-3pm	left	A lucky star.
wei	right	Good luck, but small.
3-5pm	left	Money coming.
shen	right	Someone thinking of you romantically.
5-7pm	left	A guest coming.
you	right	A guest arriving.
7-9pm	left	A guest arriving.
xu	right	A gathering or meeting.
9-11pm	left	A guest arriving.
hai	right	Gossip.

Correct for *Daylight Savings Time*, if in use (subtract one hour from the current time).

Omens from Hiccoughs	
Time	**This is an omen of:**
11pm-1am zi	A good meal and a happy dinner gathering.
1-3am chou	Someone missing you; a guest coming to seek your help.
3-5am yin	Someone missing you; a dining engagement.
5-7am mao	Wealth and happiness; someone coming to ask about a matter.
7-9am chen	A good meal; great good luck for everyone.
9-11am si	A lucky person coming to seek wealth.
11am-1pm wu	An important guest; someone wanting a dinner gathering.
1-3pm wei	Someone wanting a meal; lucky activities.
3-5pm shen	Nightmares; eating is not beneficial.
5-7pm you	Someone coming; someone asks about a matter.
7-9pm xu	Someone missing you; a meeting brings benefit.
9-11pm hai	Something frightens, but on the contrary, brings benefit.

Correct for *Daylight Savings Time*, if in use (subtract one hour from the current time).

A loving heart is true wisdom

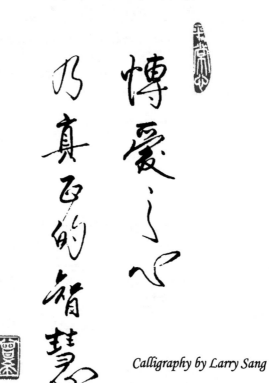

Calligraphy by Larry Sang

The Yellow Emperor

The Yellow Emperor in the Four Seasons

黄帝四季詩

Spring

Autumn

Summer

Winter

52

There is a lifetime prediction commonly found in Chinese almanacs. Based on your season of birth, find your birth time.

The Yellow Emperor in the Four Seasons

Time of Birth		Season of Birth			
		Spring February 4th to May 4th	**Summer** May 5th to August 6th	**Autumn** August 7th to November 6th	**Winter** November 7th to February 3rd
Zi	11p-1a	head	low abdomen	shoulders	low abdomen
Chou	1-3a	chest	hands	hands	knees
Yin	3-5a	feet	feet	knees	chest
Mao	5-7a	shoulders	shoulders	chest	shoulders
Chen	7-9a	knees	knees	feet	feet
Si	9-11a	hands	hands	hands	head
Wu	11a-1p	low abdomen	head	shoulders	hands
Wei	1-3p	hands	chest	chest	knees
Shen	3-5p	feet	feet	low abdomen	chest
You	5-7p	shoulders	shoulders	knees	shoulders
Xu	7-9p	knees	knees	feet	feet
Hai	9-11p	chest	chest	head	hands

Correct birth time for Daylight Saving Time, if used at the time of birth. If you were born in the Southern Hemisphere, switch the autumn and spring dates, as well as the summer and winter dates.

The Yellow Emperor in the Four Seasons

Born on the Yellow Emperor's head means a lifetime of never having worries. Even petty people have riches and honor. Clothes and food naturally come around. Your position in society is elevated, and gentlemen are good at planning. Women go through life steadily and smoothly, marrying a talented and educated person.

Born on the Yellow Emperor's hands means business capital is sufficient. Going out, you meet a benefactor. Inside the home, you have everything. Your early years are very steady and smooth. You accumulate many possesions. Wealth comes from every direction. When old, it is in your hands.

Born on the Yellow Emperor's shoulders means a life of a million riches. You have wealth in your middle years. Children and grandchildren are plenty. Clothes and income at all times are good. In old age, you have fields in the village. Siblings are helpful. Your early life is bitter, but the later end is sweet.

Born on the Yellow Emperor's chest means clothes and food are naturally ample. Experts in the pen and the sword are around you. There is music, song, and dance. Middle age brings good clothes and food. Later years are happy and prosperous. Joy, utmost honor, prosperity, and increased longevity add more blessings.

Born on the Yellow Emperor's lower abdomen, you were treasured by your parents. In middle age, clothes and food are good. When old you obtain gold. The family reputation is changing a lot. You are a noble person. Children and grandchildren must newly shine. Cultured and bright, they advance a lot.

Born on the Yellow Emperor's knees means doing things is without benefit. In your early years, you toiled a lot, but did not lack clothes and food. Every day, you travel on the road; you cannot avoid running back and forth. Old age is smooth, with honor and prosperity, but in middle age, hard work is extreme.

Born on the Yellow Emperor's feet, practice moral teachings to avoid toil. A lifetime that is safe and sound, but unsuitable to reside in your ancestor's home. Women marry two husbands. Men have two wives. Search lonely mountain ranges. Leave your homeland to achieve good fortune.

Feng Shui

Feng Shui

Makes the Universe Work for You

We live in a universe that is filled with different energies. Our planet rotates on its axis, creating cycles of day and night. The earth also revolves around the sun in yearly cycles and is subject to various gravitational and magnetic fields. Our solar system is moving through space and is also subject to other forces in the universe. These physical forces and many different time cycles affect us profoundly. The Chinese have spent centuries observing the effects of these forces, and learning how to better harmonize humans with their environment. This is the science and art of Feng Shui (Chinese geomancy).

Feng Shui uses observation, repeatable calculations and methodologies, and is based on the study of the environment, both inside and out of the house. Feng Shui can help you determine the best home to live in, which colors can enhance your home, the best bed positions for deep sleep, and how to change your business or home into a center of power. Feng Shui can help improve your health, your relationships and your prosperity. It is based on a complex calculation and observation of the environment, rather than a metaphysical reading relying on inspiration or intuition.

The American Feng Shui Institute publishes the annual Chinese Astrology and Feng Shui Guide so that both the Feng Shui professional and layperson can benefit from the knowledge of the incoming energy cycles and their influences. With this knowledge, one can adjust their environment to make it as harmonious as possible for the current year.

The following sections contain the energy patterns for the current year with an analysis and remedy for each of the eight directions. For the nonprofessional, there is a section on how to prepare your home for this reading. Please note that Feng Shui is a deep and complex science that requires many years to master. Preparing your home to receive the annual energy is one aspect that anyone can apply. A professional reading is recommended to anyone who wishes to receive the greatest benefits possible that Feng Shui can bring.

Preparing your home for a Feng Shui reading

The Floor Plan

The first requirement for preparing your home for a Feng Shui annual reading is to create a proportional floor plan. This plan can be hand drawn or be the original building plans, as long as the plan is proportionally correct. It is not necessary to draw in all your furniture except perhaps noting your bed and desk. It is important that you indicate where all window and door openings are.

Example A
Floor plan

Example B
Floor plan

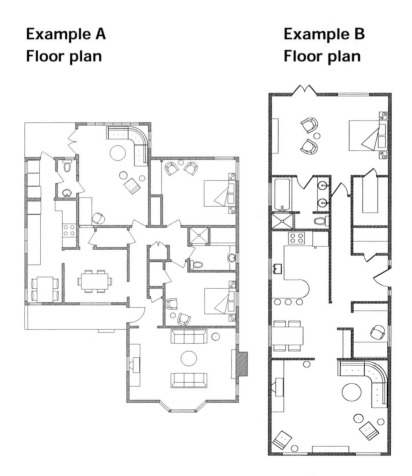

Preparing your home for a Feng Shui reading

Gridding The Floor Plan

Once you have your floor plan drawn, you then overlay a 9- square grid. This grid is proportional to the floor plan. If it were a long and narrow house, so would the grid be long and narrow. You want to divide the floor plan into equal thirds both top to bottom and left to right as shown below:

Example A
with grid

Example B
with grid

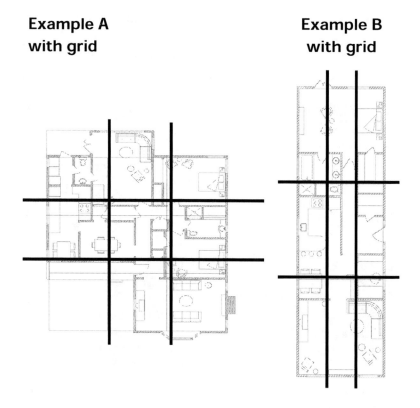

The Compass Reading

The next step is to determine the alignment of your house with the earth magnetic fields by taking a compass reading. It is very important to take an accurate reading and not guess the orientation based on the direction of the sun or a map.

Why Do You Need To Use A Compass?

In Feng Shui, we look at the eight cardinal and inter-cardinal directions: East, Southeast, South, Southwest, West, Northwest, North, and Northeast when analyzing a home or building. Each of these directions holds unique significance to these buildings. If you do not use a compass to determine the correct orientation, you might completely misread your home. You cannot map the qi within the building without an exact orientation. It is similar to finding your way out of a forest without a compass. You have a high probability of getting lost. Without a compass, it simply is not Feng Shui.

A Compass vs. A Luopan

You can use any compass if you do not have a Luopan. The Luopan is simply a Chinese compass that helps determine the sitting direction of a building. It also contains a wealth of information on its dial that is used for more advanced applications. In recent years, Master Larry Sang simplified the traditional Luopan specifically for training Western students. Although it looks simple compared to an original Luopan, it has all the tools you need to accurately analyze a building. An important fact to remember about a Luopan is that it points to the South. The following information and instructions apply to a Luopan, however, if you are using a Western compass these concepts are easy to adapt.

Sang's Luopan

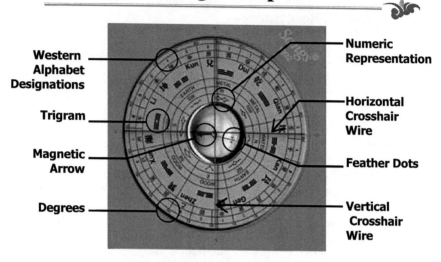

Western Alphabet Designations

Trigram

Magnetic Arrow

Degrees

Numeric Representation

Horizontal Crosshair Wire

Feather Dots

Vertical Crosshair Wire

Parts of Sang's Luopan

The Magnetic Arrow - The arrowhead points South rather than North. Western compasses point North.

The Feather Dots - (The twin dots at the center of the rotating dial). Always adjust the rotating (gold) dial to align the twin dots with the feather end of the arrow.

The Numeric Representations - The innermost ring has a dot pattern that represents the Trigrams' numbers. For example, Kun has two dots and Qian has six dots.

Crosshair Alignments - The red crosshairs designate the facing and sitting directions. Once the arrow is steady and the feather end is aligned over the north twin dots, you can determine the sitting direction and the facing direction.

The Eight Trigrams - The Eight Trigrams are the basis for orientation in Feng Shui and are shown on the Luopan with their respective elements, symbols, and directions.

Western Alphabet Designations - Each Trigram is divided into three equal parts. These parts are shown with both their Chinese symbols and using the Western Alphabet.

The Degrees - Outermost on the dial are the Western compass degrees in Arabic numerals.

General Guidelines for using the Luopan:

To use the Luopan or compass correctly, remember the following guidelines:

1. Always stand straight and upright.

2. Do not wear metal jewelry or belt buckles that can skew the compass.

3. Avoid any electrical influences such as automobiles or electrical boxes.

4. Always stand parallel to the building.

5. Keep your feet square below you.

6. You can keep the Luopan in the lower box case to manage it better.

Taking a reading with the Luopan:

With the general guidelines for using a luopan in mind, now you are ready to take a reading to determine which wall or corner of your home is located closest to North.

1. Take your reading outside, standing parallel to your home with your back to it. Stand straight and hold the Luopan at waist level. Wait until the arrow ceases to quiver.

2. Slowly turn the center (gold) dial so that the North/feather dots align with the feather of the arrow. If using a Western compass, turn the compass so that the needle's arrow end aligns with north (between 337.5 - 22.5 degrees).

3. Please take at least three separate readings from other positions. If you find that there is a discrepancy, take various readings at various locations until you are sure which one is correct. One direction should stand out as being correct.

4. Indicate on your floor plan which section is North. Fill in the other directions as illustrated. Please note that North can lie in a corner section.

Example A   **Example B**

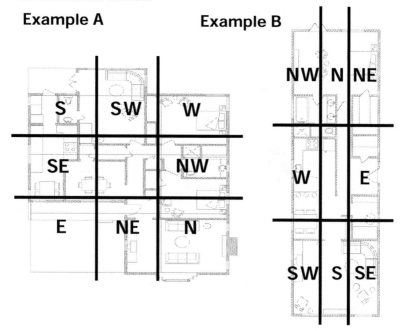

Directions to Avoid for Construction

The Three Sha and the Sui Po   2010

The **Three Sha** are in the **North (Northwest and Northeast):**

North (Northwest and Northeast):

Hai, Zi and **Chou** directions.

The **Sui Po** or **Year Breaker** is in the **Southwest Shen** direction.

The **Tai Sui** is in the **Northeast: Yin** direction.

> Therefore, avoid using these directions:
> **Hai, Zi, Chou, Yin, and Shen**

Directions to Avoid

15° Direction	Degrees	45° Direction	Sang's Luopan Alpha Designation
Hai		NW	w
Ren			x
Zi	322.5° - 37.5°	N	a
Gui			b
Chou		NE	c
Yin	52.5° - 67.5°		e
Shen	232.5° - 247.5°	SW	q

What should we avoid in these directions?

➤ New construction sitting in these directions (except Yin Northeast).

➤ Major renovation to buildings sitting in these directions (except Yin Northeast).

➤ Major renovation to this section of the house, regardless of the sitting direction.

➤ Burial of the deceased in these directions.

➤ Digging or breaking of earth in these directions. If digging cannot be avoided in any of these areas, then place a metal wind chime outside between the house and the digging site.

➤ In addition, Tigers or Monkeys born in the first, fourth, or seventh month of the lunar calendar should avoid attending funerals or burials.

Feng Shui 2010

Qi Pattern

SE ☷☳ 7 Red	S ☵ 3 Jade	SW ☶ 5 Yellow
E ☳ 6 White	8 White	W ☱ 1 White
NE ☶ 2 Black	N ☵ 4 Green	NW ☰ 9 Purple

The Qi (energy) shift begins on

February 4th, 2010 at 06:42 am

Introduction

While this diagram may look foreign to the beginner, it is essential information for the experienced Feng Shui practitioner. Each year the qi pattern brings different effects. Some of these effects are quite auspicious and favorable and some may be inauspicious and not so favorable.

The effects of the 2010 energy pattern are analyzed for you in the following pages. Each analysis contains suggested remedies or enhancements for each section. Remedies are recommended to reduce negative qi. Enhancements are recommended to increase beneficial qi. These remedies or enhancements consist of the five elements: wood, fire, earth, metal, and water.

To use a remedy or enhancement, it must be placed inside the house within that particular section. If more than one room exists within a section, then each room needs to have its own remedy or enhancement. Any exceptions will be noted.

Feng Shui 2010

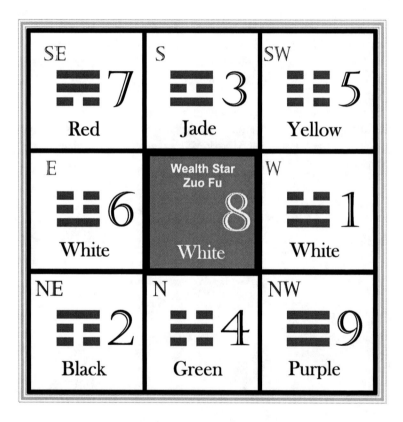

SE **7** Red	S **3** Jade	SW **5** Yellow
E **6** White	Wealth Star Zuo Fu **8** White	W **1** White
NE **2** Black	N **4** Green	NW **9** Purple

The Center Section

Center

Analysis

Last year in this chapter, we discussed that Fire above Mountain forms Hexagram 56, Lu. "The meaning of this hexagram is 'Traveling: On a journey, only minor undertakings go well.' ... People will experience global hyperinflation ahead. All the governments around the world can do very little about it."

In 2010 the **8 White Zuo Fu Star** visits the center. We are currently in Period 8; because the same star, 8 White (earth), is in the center, we can predict that this year the world enters an era of "slower growth." Our economic recovery could be slow and painful.

8 White corresponds to the Gen trigram in the *Yi Jing*. Gen represents the Mountain. The **8 White** Star, Mountain, above and below forms hexagram 52, Gen. The meaning of this hexagram is "Keeping still. Impediment" The image is vivid: The virtue of Mountain is its stillness. The double mountain represents an insurmountable blockage which necessitates stillness. Therefore, the recovery of global economy is expected to be much more subdued than might normally be the case.

However, the **8 White Zuo Fu Star** is a wealth star. Visiting the center in 2010, it presents an optimistic outlook. The global economy can be expected to emerge slowly from recession in the second half of 2010.

Feng Shui 2010

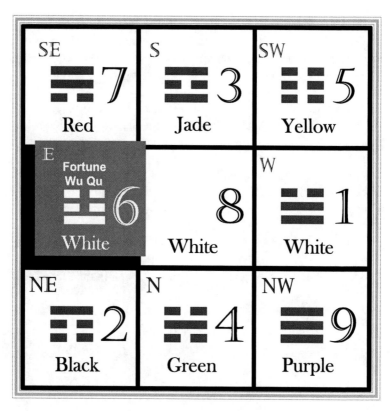

SE	S	SW
☷ 7 Red	☱ 3 Jade	☶ 5 Yellow
E Fortune Wu Qu ☳ 6 White	8 White	**W** ☵ 1 White
NE ☶ 2 Black	N ☴ 4 Green	NW ☰ 9 Purple

The East Section

East

Situation

Doors, bedrooms, or study rooms in the east section.

Analysis

The *6 White Wu Qu Fortune Star* visits the east in 2010. The 6 White Star's element is metal and it is a fortune star. The east section is the home of the *3 Jade Lu Cun Star,* which belongs to the wood element. The combination of the wood of 3 Jade and the metal of 6 White create a 3-6 combination, a domination relationship. It brings both promotion and money prospects. Yet, since metal dominates wood, there is the potential of leg injuries or throat discomfort if someone stays in this area more than eight hours per day as an office or bedroom.

Remedy

Use water element as a remedy in this section. A fountain or aquarium in the east will help change the poison into medicine.

After Remedy

Beneficial for business expansion and promotion, as well as for people who work in speech-related professions such as politicians, sales, or wood and water related businesses.

Feng Shui

2010

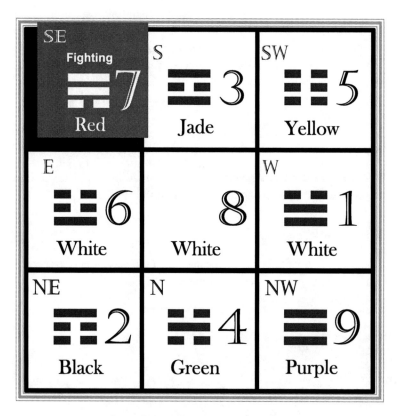

SE **Fighting** 7 Red	S 3 Jade	SW 5 Yellow
E 6 White	8 White	W 1 White
NE 2 Black	N 4 Green	NW 9 Purple

The Southeast Section

Southeast

Situation

Doors, bedrooms, study rooms in the southeast section.

Analysis

The *7 Po Jun Fighting Star* visits the southeast in 2010. The 7 Red Star is metal element. It is a competitive and fighting star. The southeast section is the home of the *4 Green Wen Qu Literary Star*, which is wood element. The combination of the wood of 4 Green and the metal of 7 Red creates a domination relationship. This makes the southeast section not beneficial for artists, writers and people working in the entertainment business. There is also the potential of thigh injuries or waist pain. Moreover, if a female's bedroom is in this section, she easily receives some kind of cheating heart romance. However, using the water element can change the above mentioned negativity into positive qi.

Caution

Not beneficial for artists, writers and people working in the entertainment business, and it easily brings unhappy romance.

Remedy

Use the water element as a remedy in this section. A fountain or aquarium in the southeast will help change the poison into medicine.

After Remedy

It will bring strong romantic qi (Peach Blossom) and good results in academia for students, writers, and people working in the entertainment industry.

Feng Shui 2010

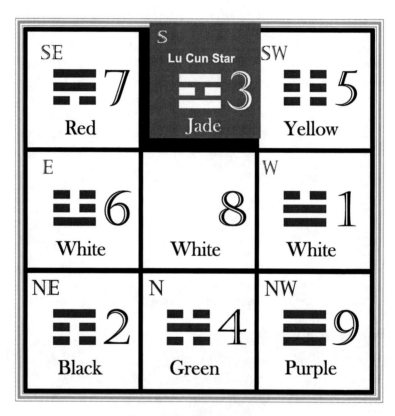

	S	
SE ☷ **7** Red	**Lu Cun Star** ☳ **3** Jade	**SW** ☶ **5** Yellow
E ☴ **6** White	**8** White	**W** ☱ **1** White
NE ☵ **2** Black	**N** ☲ **4** Green	**NW** ☰ **9** Purple

The South Section

South

Situation

Doors, bedrooms, study rooms in the south section.

Analysis

This year the *3 Jade Lu Cun Star* falls in the south. The 3 Jade Star is wood element. It represents ambition, expansion, promotions, gossip, arguments, misunderstandings, and robberies. The south is the home base of the *9 Purple Celebration Star*. It is fire element. Fire and wood create a harmonious relationship. Make use of this section which is beneficial for career expansion, development, and sales or promotion. It will bring in things to celebrate, such as a new life partner, marriage, job promotion, or receiving some kind of special honor. However, be on guard for a break in or lawsuit.

Benefits

For career expansion, development, and sales or promotion.

Caution

Not beneficial for jewelers, goldsmiths, or metal related businesses. If this section is the main entrance, be on guard for robbery, fighting or legal problems.

Feng Shui 2010

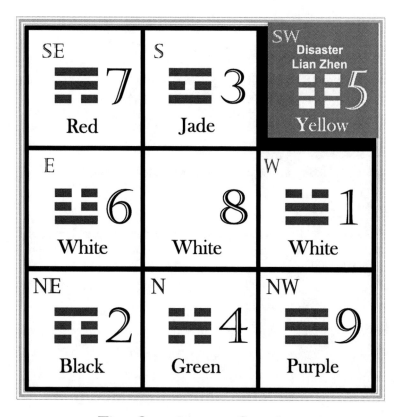

SE **7** Red	S **3** Jade	SW Disaster Lian Zhen **5** Yellow
E **6** White	**8** White	W **1** White
NE **2** Black	N **4** Green	NW **9** Purple

The Southwest Section

Southwest

Situation

Doors, bedrooms, study rooms in the southwest section.

Analysis

This year the *5 Yellow Lian Zhen Disaster Star* falls in the southwest. This inauspicious star brings the potential for delays, obstacles, fire, lawsuits, sickness, and casualties. The 5 yellow star is earth element. The southwest section is the home of the *2 Black Ju Men Star*. The 2 Black Star represents sickness, gossip and misunderstanding. The 2 Black Star is also earth element. Both direction and star are of the same element. The 2-5 combination makes the southwest a critical section in the year of the Tiger. If the main entrance or bedroom is unfortunately located in this section and no remedy is applied, an unexpected casualty is quite possible. It is advisable to avoid spending a lot of time in this area. In the southwest section, ground digging should especially be avoided to prevent the occurrence of misfortune.

Remedy

To reduce the above mentioned potential negative effects, use the metal element as a remedy in this section. A metal remedy can consist of metal décor such as a piece of sculpture. An ornament that has moving metal parts is preferable, such as a grandfather clock.

Caution

Do not allow construction or ground digging.

Feng Shui 2010

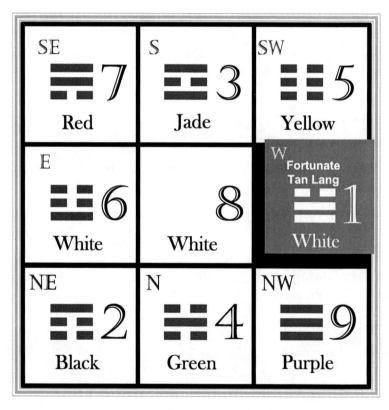

SE **7** Red	S **3** Jade	SW **5** Yellow
E **6** White	**8** White	W **Fortunate Tan Lang 1** White
NE **2** Black	N **4** Green	NW **9** Purple

The West Section

West

Situation

Doors, bedrooms, study rooms in the west section.

Analysis

The *1 White Tan Lang Fortunate Star* is in the northwest this year.
Its element is water. This Fortunate Star brings wealth, fame, romance,
and benefit from negotiation. The west is the home of the *7 Red Star*,
which is metal element and has an aggressive fighting nature. Water
and metal are in a production relationship, and with auspicious stars
such as Long De and Zi Wei gathering here, this section is strong in
peach blossom and money luck. It will be quite beneficial for bankers,
loan officers, public relationships, water related businesses and the
entertainment industry (bars, nightclubs and casinos). It also will be
beneficial for the self-employed to expand their business.

Benefits

Beneficial for bankers, loan officers, public relationships, water
related businesses and the entertainment industry (bars, nightclubs
and casinos). Strong for Peach Blossom.

Caution

Conflicts, arguments and misunderstandings are easily aroused.

Feng Shui

2010

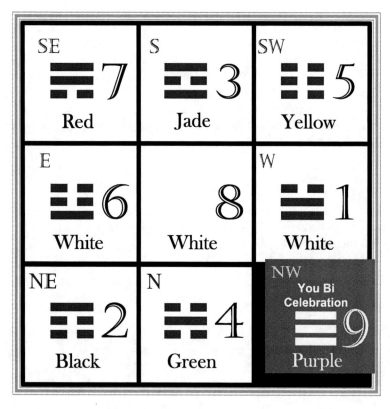

SE ▤7 Red	**S** ▤3 Jade	**SW** ▥5 Yellow
E ▤6 White	8 White	**W** ▤1 White
NE ▤2 Black	**N** ▤4 Green	**NW** You Bi Celebration ▤9 Purple

The Northwest Section

Northwest

Situation

Doors, bedrooms, study rooms in the northwest section.

Analysis

The *9 Purple You Bi Celebration Star* is in the northwest section this year. This 9 Purple Star represents wealth, fame, promotion and celebration. The element of the 9 Purple Star is fire. The northwest is the home of the *6 White Fortune Star*, which is metal element. The domination relationship of fire and metal make this section good and bad luck mixed. The 9 Purple Star in the northwest enhances the home of the 6 White Fortune Star, turning it into a wealth-making and power-enhancing section. Yet this year, the northwest section is under the influence of the inauspicious star Jie Sha (Robbery); if the main entrance or bedroom falls in this section, be careful of conflict with others, mostly due to challenges to the power of authority. Also be on guard for unexpected casualty or break in.

Caution

Conflicts, arguments and misunderstandings are easily aroused, challenging the power of authorities.

Remedy

To reduce the potential negative effects, use the earth element as a remedy. This can be a decorative piece of glazed pottery or porcelain.

Feng Shui 2010

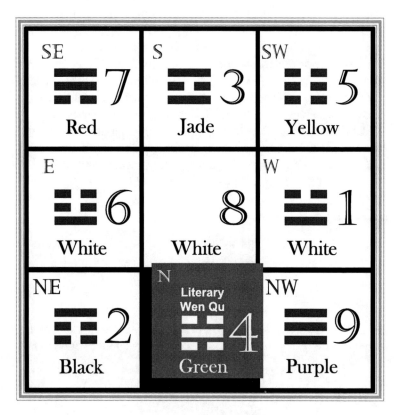

SE ䷲ 7 Red	**S** ䷲ 3 Jade	**SW** ䷲ 5 Yellow
E ䷲ 6 White	8 White	**W** ䷲ 1 White
NE ䷲ 2 Black	**N** Literary Wen Qu ䷲ 4 Green	**NW** ䷲ 9 Purple

The North Section

North

Situation

Doors, bedrooms, study rooms in the north section.

Analysis

This year the *4 Green Wen Qu Literary Star* falls in the north. This star represents creative and academic achievements and Peach Blossom. The 4 Green Star's element is wood. The north is the home of the *1 White Fortune Star*, and is water element. The 1 White (water) and the 4 Green (wood) are in a productive relationship. The combination of 1 - 4 makes this section very strong in peach blossom for the female owner, and beneficial for literature, scholars, writers, actors, students, merchants, and water-related industries. However, there are number of inauspicious stars gathering with the Disaster Sha in the north, making it an unfavorable section during the year of the Tiger, 2010. To prevent the occurrence of misfortune, it is inadvisable to dig in the earth or do construction inside or outside the house in the north.

Benefits

Beneficial for literature, scholars, writers, actors, students, and merchants. Beneficial for seeking life partners and marriage proposals.

Caution

Do not allow construction or ground digging.

feng shui

Feng Shui 2010

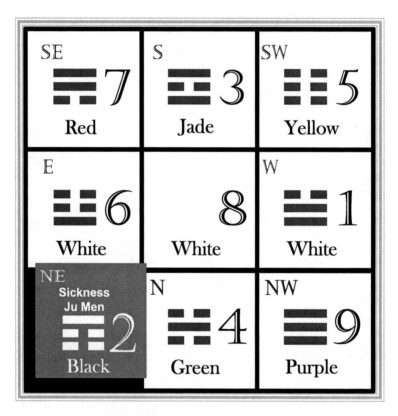

SE	S	SW
7 Red	3 Jade	5 Yellow
E 6 White	8 White	W 1 White
NE Sickness Ju Men 2 Black	N 4 Green	NW 9 Purple

The Northeast Section

Northeast

Situation

Doors, bedrooms, study rooms in the northeast section.

Analysis

The *2 Black Ju Men Star* visits the northwest section this year. Its element is earth. This 2 Black Star is beneficial for medicine, doctors, attorneys and women's rights. But the 2 Black Star also represents sickness, gossip and misunderstanding in the current Period 8 (from 2004 to 2023). The northeast is the home of the *8 White Zuo Fu Money Star* which brings fame and wealth. Its element is earth. The two earths are the same element. The inauspicious yearly Sui Sha Star also falls in the northeast together with the Tai Sui. If the main entrance is in this section, it is not advisable to make any kind of risky investment or career switch. A bedroom in this section is not beneficial for teenagers or pregnant women. There is also the potential of bone pain or injury to the four limbs. Due to the Tai Sui Star meeting the Sui Sha Star, ground digging should strictly be avoided.

Caution

Not beneficial for pregnant women or teenagers. Avoid digging in this section to prevent unhappy things from occurring.

Remedy

Try to keep this area always clean and bright. **No digging in the ground!**

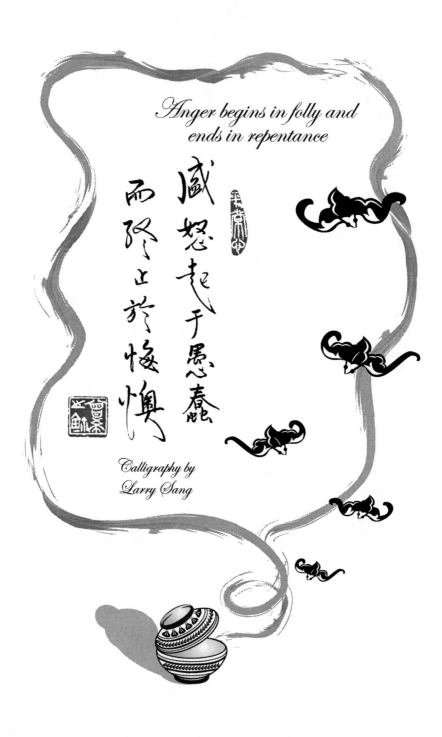

Anger begins in folly and
ends in repentance

Calligraphy by
Larry Sang

Day Selection

Day Selection

Introduction to Day Selection

Day Selection has been used for a long time in China. Every year, almanacs would be published giving the best days for important activities, as well as days to avoid. It is thought that a positive outcome is more likely when an activity is begun on an auspicious day. In English, we talk about getting things off to a good start, but have no particular methodology to do this.

There are three aspects to selecting a good day: picking a day that is good for the activity, avoiding a day that is bad for the activity, and picking a day that is not bad for the person(s) involved. In the calendar pages that follow, each day will list two or three activities that are auspicious or inauspicious on that day. If you wanted to pick a date to get married, you would first look for days that were considered good for weddings. In addition, you need to check the birth information of the bride and groom. If the bride is a Rabbit and the groom is a Rat, then you also need to avoid any days that say Bad for Rat or Bad for Rabbit, even if they are good for weddings in general.

In addition, there are some days that are not good for any important activity. Usually this is because the energy of heaven and earth is too strong or inharmonious on those days.

Day Selection is used for the first day of an activity. It does not affect a continued activity. For example, you should begin construction on a day that is good for groundbreaking, but it is not a problem if the construction is continued through a day that is bad for groundbreaking. The construction need not be stopped.

On the next page are definitions of the various activities included in Master Sang's Day Selection Calendar.

Calender Terminology Key

Animals:
Generally a bad day for a person born in the year of the animal listed. Even if an activity is listed as beneficial for that day, it will usually not be beneficial for that animal.

Begin Mission:
Beginning a new position, mission, or assignment.

Burial:
Burial.

Business:
Trade or business.

Buy Property:
Purchasing real estate.

Contracts:
Signing or entering into a contract, pact, or agreement.

Don't Do Important things:
A bad day for most activities.

Fix House:
Repairing the inside or outside of the house. Also for installing major appliances, such as the stove or oven.

Funeral:
Funerals.

Ground Breaking:
Beginning construction or disturbing the earth.

Healing:
Curing diseases, beginning a course of treatment.

Lawsuits:
Filing a lawsuit or going to court.

Moving:
Moving or changing residences.

Planting:
Gardening or planting.

Prayer:
Praying for blessings or happiness.

School:
Admissions into a new school.

Travel:
Going out or beginning a trip.

Wedding:
Marriage ceremonies or becoming engaged to be married.

Worship:
Rituals, rites, ceremonies, offering sacrifices, or honoring ancestors or the dead.

January 2010

Unfavorable for:

Day		Unfavorable for
Fri 1	⊖ **DON'T DO IMPORTANT THINGS** ⊖	*Snake*
Sat 2	**Good for:** Prayer, worship ***Bad for:*** *Grand opening, ground breaking, wedding*	*Horse*
Sun 3	**Good for:** Grand opening, moving, wedding ***Bad for:*** *Burial, ground breaking*	*Sheep*
Mon 4	**Good for:** Ground breaking, grand opening, begin mission ***Bad for:*** *Lawsuit*	*Monkey*
Tue 5	**Good for:** Grand opening, moving, wedding ***Bad for:*** *Burial, funeral*	*Rooster*
Wed 6	**Good for:** Worship ***Bad for:*** *Burial, grand opening, wedding*	*Dog*
Thu 7	⊖ **DON'T DO IMPORTANT THINGS** ⊖	*Pig*
Fri 8	**Good for:** Prayer, worship ***Bad for:*** *Business, grand opening, wedding*	*Rat*
Sat 9	⊖ **DON'T DO IMPORTANT THINGS** ⊖	*Ox*
Sun 10	**Good for:** Business, contract, grand opening ***Bad for:*** *Fix house, ground breaking*	*Tiger*
Mon 11	**Good for:** Grand opening, moving, wedding ***Bad for:*** *Lawsuit, funeral*	*Rabbit*
Tue 12	**Good for:** Prayer, worship ***Bad for:*** *Grand opening, wedding*	*Dragon*
Wed 13	**Good for:** Prayer, school ***Bad for:*** *Business, grand opening, wedding*	*Snake*
Thu 14	**Good for:** Burial, ground breaking, worship ***Bad for:*** *Begin mission, grand opening*	*Horse*
Fri 15	**Good for:** Prayer, worship ***Bad for:*** *Grand opening, wedding*	*Sheep*

Day		Zodiac
Sat **16**	**Good for:** Worship *Bad for: Grand opening, travel, moving*	*Monkey*
Sun **17**	**Good for:** Prayer, worship *Bad for: Grand opening, ground breaking*	*Rooster*
Mon **18**	⊖ **DON'T DO IMPORTANT THINGS** ⊖	*Dog*
Tue **19**	**Good for:** Fix house, ground breaking, wedding *Bad for: Fix house, moving*	*Pig*
Wed **20**	**Good for:** Grand opening, moving, wedding *Bad for: Burial, funeral*	*Rat*
Thu **21**	⊖ **DON'T DO IMPORTANT THINGS** ⊖	*Ox*
Fri **22**	**Good for:** Prayer, worship *Bad for: Business, buy property, grand opening*	*Tiger*
Sat **23**	**Good for:** Grand opening, contract, wedding *Bad for: Fix house, lawsuit*	*Rabbit*
Sun **24**	**Good for:** Prayer, worship *Bad for: Ground breaking, wedding*	*Dragon*
Mon **25**	**Good for:** Grand opening, enter school, ground breaking *Bad for: Lawsuit*	*Snake*
Tue **26**	**Good for:** Prayer, worship *Bad for: Grand opening, wedding*	*Horse*
Wed **27**	⊖ **DON'T DO IMPORTANT THINGS** ⊖	*Sheep*
Thu **28**	**Good for:** Worship *Bad for: Business, wedding*	*Monkey*
Fri **29**	**Good for:** Grand opening, business, wedding *Bad for: Lawsuit*	*Rooster*
Sat **30**	**Good for:** Prayer, worship *Bad for: Grand opening, wedding*	*Dog*
Sun **31**	**Good for:** Business, ground breaking, moving *Bad for: Fix house, lawsuit*	*Pig*

February 2010

Unfavorable for:

Mon **1**	**Good for:** Contracts, prayer, worship *Bad for: Grand opening, begin mission, moving*	*Rat*
Tue **2**	⊖ **DON'T DO IMPORTANT THINGS** ⊖	*Ox*
Wed **3**	⊖ **DON'T DO IMPORTANT THINGS** ⊖	*Tiger*
Thu **4**	**Good for:** Business, contracts, ground breaking *Bad for: Travel, moving, wedding*	*Rabbit*
Fri **5**	**Good for:** Ground breaking, school, healing *Bad for: Lawsuit, moving*	*Dragon*
Sat **6**	**Good for:** Grand opening, wedding, contracts *Bad for: Moving, burial*	*Snake*
Sun **7**	**Good for:** Business, contracts *Bad for: Burial, ground breaking*	*Horse*
Mon **8**	**Good for:** Prayer, worship *Bad for: Business, burial*	*Sheep*
Tue **9**	**Good for:** Begin mission, school *Bad for: Ground breaking, wedding*	*Monkey*
Wed **10**	**Good for:** Moving, wedding *Bad for: Burial, funeral*	*Rooster*
Thu **11**	**Good for:** Begin mission, grand opening, wedding *Bad for: Funeral, ground breaking*	*Dog*
Fri **12**	⊖ **DON'T DO IMPORTANT THINGS** ⊖	*Pig*
Sat **13**	**Good for:** Grand opening, wedding, contracts *Bad for: Lawsuit, buy property*	*Rat*
Sun **14**	⊖ **DON'T DO IMPORTANT THINGS** ⊖	*Ox*

Mon **15**	⊖ **DON'T DO IMPORTANT THINGS** ⊖	*Tiger*
Tue **16**	**Good for:** Ground breaking, wedding, business *Bad for: Fix house, moving*	*Rabbit*
Wed **17**	**Good for:** Prayer, worship *Bad for: Ground opening, lawsuit*	*Dragon*
Thu **18**	**Good for:** Grand opening, wedding, contracts *Bad for: Burial, funeral*	*Snake*
Fri **19**	**Good for:** Business school, begin mission *Bad for: Lawsuit, ground breaking*	*Horse*
Sat **20**	**Good for:** Prayer, burial *Bad for: Moving, wedding*	*Sheep*
Sun **21**	**Good for:** Business, contracts *Bad for: Moving, wedding*	*Monkey*
Mon **22**	**Good for:** Prayer, burial *Bad for: Begin mission, grand opening*	*Rooster*
Tue **23**	**Good for:** Prayer, worship *Bad for: Ground breaking, moving*	*Dog*
Wed **24**	**Good for:** Worship *Bad for: Grand opening, wedding*	*Pig*
Thu **25**	**Good for:** Business, wedding, contracts *Bad for: Burial, funeral*	*Rat*
Fri **26**	**Good for:** Fix house, moving, ground breaking *Bad for: Lawsuit, wedding*	*Ox*
Sat **27**	⊖ **DON'T DO IMPORTANT THINGS** ⊖	*Tiger*
Sun **28**	**Good for:** Burial, ground breaking, funeral *Bad for: Grand opening, begin mission*	*Rabbit*

S	M	T	W	T	F	S
	1	2	3	4	5	6
7	8	9	10	11	12	13
14	15	16	17	18	19	20
21	22	23	24	25	26	27
28	29	30	31			

March 2010

Unfavorable for:

Mon **1**	**Good for:** Prayer, worship *Bad for: Contracts, wedding*	*Dragon*
Tue **2**	**Good for:** Begin mission, grand opening, wedding *Bad for: Burial, funeral*	*Snake*
Wed **3**	**Good for:** Grand opening, wedding, business *Bad for: Funeral, ground breaking*	*Horse*
Thu **4**	**Good for:** Prayer, worship *Bad for: Grand opening, begin mission, wedding*	*Sheep*
Fri **5**	**Good for:** Prayer, business *Bad for: Moving, wedding*	*Monkey*
Sat **6**	**Good for:** Begin mission, travel *Bad for: Ground breaking, wedding*	*Rooster*
Sun **7**	**Good for:** Fix house, ground breaking *Bad for: Contracts, buy property*	*Dog*
Mon **8**	**Good for:** Business, contracts, grand opening *Bad for: Burial, ground breaking*	*Pig*
Tue **9**	**Good for:** Prayer, worship *Bad for: Grand opening, wedding*	*Rat*
Wed **10**	**Good for:** Begin mission, moving, buy property *Bad for: Ground breaking, planting*	*Ox*
Thu **11**	⊖ **DON'T DO IMPORTANT THINGS** ⊖	*Tiger*
Fri **12**	⊖ **DON'T DO IMPORTANT THINGS** ⊖	*Rabbit*
Sat **13**	**Good for:** Prayer, worship *Bad for: Grand opening, moving, wedding*	*Dragon*
Sun **14**	**Good for:** School, grand opening *Bad for: Lawsuit, moving*	*Snake*
Mon **15**	**Good for:** Worship, prayer *Bad for: Moving, wedding*	*Horse*

Tue **16**	**Good for:** Grand opening, contracts, wedding *Bad for: Burial, ground breaking*	*Sheep*
Wed **17**	**Good for:** Burial, prayer *Bad for: Travel, wedding*	*Monkey*
Thu **18**	**Good for:** Begin mission, business, contracts *Bad for: Ground breaking, wedding*	*Rooster*
Fri **19**	**Good for:** Grand opening, business *Bad for: Burial, funeral*	*Dog*
Sat **20**	⊖ **DON'T DO IMPORTANT THINGS** ⊖	*Pig*
Sun **21**	**Good for:** Prayer, worship *Bad for: Grand opening, ground breaking, wedding*	*Rat*
Mon **22**	**Good for:** Fix house, ground breaking *Bad for: Lawsuit, wedding*	*Ox*
Tue **23**	⊖ **DON'T DO IMPORTANT THINGS** ⊖	*Tiger*
Wed **24**	⊖ **DON'T DO IMPORTANT THINGS** ⊖	*Rabbit*
Thu **25**	**Good for:** Begin mission, grand opening, wedding *Bad for: Burial, funeral*	*Dragon*
Fri **26**	**Good for:** Fix house, ground breaking *Bad for: Grand opening, wedding*	*Snake*
Sat **27**	**Good for:** Prayer *Bad for: Begin mission, grand opening, wedding*	*Horse*
Sun **28**	**Good for:** Business, contracts, wedding *Bad for: Burial, ground breaking*	*Sheep*
Mon **29**	**Good for:** Burial, ground breaking *Bad for: Buy property, moving*	*Monkey*
Tue **30**	**Good for:** Prayer, burial *Bad for: Moving, wedding*	*Rooster*
Wed **31**	**Good for:** Prayer, worship *Bad for: Begin mission, grand opening*	*Dog*

S	M	T	W	T	F	S
				1	2	3
4	5	6	7	8	9	10
11	12	13	14	15	16	17
18	19	20	21	22	23	24
25	26	27	28	29	30	31

April 2010

Unfavorable for:

Thu 1	**Good for:** Business, contracts, grand opening *Bad for:* Ground breaking, moving	*Pig*
Fri 2	**Good for:** Prayer *Bad for:* Ground breaking, planting	*Rat*
Sat 3	**Good for:** Fix house, moving, ground breaking *Bad for:* Contracts, lawsuit	*Ox*
Sun 4	⊖ **DON'T DO IMPORTANT THINGS** ⊖	*Tiger*
Mon 5	**Good for:** Contracts, wedding *Bad for:* Funeral, moving	*Rabbit*
Tue 6	⊖ **DON'T DO IMPORTANT THINGS** ⊖	*Dragon*
Wed 7	**Good for:** Begin mission, fix house, moving *Bad for:* Funeral, ground breaking	*Snake*
Thu 8	**Good for:** Grand opening, school, wedding *Bad for:* Lawsuit, moving	*Horse*
Fri 9	**Good for:** Prayer, worship *Bad for:* Burial, grand opening	*Sheep*
Sat 10	**Good for:** Grand opening, school, wedding *Bad for:* Burial, ground breaking	*Monkey*
Sun 11	**Good for:** Prayer, burial *Bad for:* Wedding, moving	*Rooster*
Mon 12	**Good for:** Prayer, worship *Bad for:* Grand opening, ground breaking	*Dog*
Tue 13	**Good for:** Prayer, worship *Bad for:* Healing, moving, ground breaking	*Pig*
Wed 14	**Good for:** Business, school *Bad for:* Ground breaking, travel	*Rat*
Thu 15	**Good for:** Fix house, prayer *Bad for:* Grand opening, wedding	*Ox*

Fri **16**	⊖ **DON'T DO IMPORTANT THINGS** ⊖	*Tiger*
Sat **17**	**Good for:** Grand opening, wedding, begin mission ***Bad for:*** *Ground breaking, fix house*	*Rabbit*
Sun **18**	⊖ **DON'T DO IMPORTANT THINGS** ⊖	*Dragon*
Mon **19**	**Good for:** Prayer, planting ***Bad for:*** *Grand opening, wedding*	*Snake*
Tue **20**	**Good for:** Begin mission, grand opening, wedding ***Bad for:*** *Lawsuit, moving*	*Horse*
Wed **21**	**Good for:** Prayer, worship ***Bad for:*** *Burial, ground breaking*	*Sheep*
Thu **22**	**Good for:** Prayer ***Bad for:*** *Ground breaking, wedding*	*Monkey*
Fri **23**	**Good for:** Prayer, burial ***Bad for:*** *Travel, wedding*	*Rooster*
Sat **24**	**Good for:** Begin mission, travel ***Bad for:*** *Ground breaking, wedding*	*Dog*
Sun **25**	**Good for:** Prayer, worship ***Bad for:*** *Begin mission, grand opening, moving*	*Pig*
Mon **26**	**Good for:** Business, school ***Bad for:*** *Ground breaking, lawsuit*	*Rat*
Tue **27**	**Good for:** Business, contracts, school ***Bad for:*** *Burial, moving*	*Ox*
Wed **28**	⊖ **DON'T DO IMPORTANT THINGS** ⊖	*Tiger*
Thu **29**	**Good for:** Wedding, grand opening, begin mission ***Bad for:*** *Ground breaking, moving*	*Rabbit*
Fri **30**	⊖ **DON'T DO IMPORTANT THINGS** ⊖	*Dragon*

S	M	T	W	T	F	S
						1
2	3	4	5	6	7	8
9	10	11	12	13	14	15
16	17	18	19	20	21	22
23	24	25	26	27	28	29
30	31					

May 2010

Unfavorable for:

Sat **1**	**Good for:** Begin mission, business *Bad for:* Funeral, ground breaking	*Snake*
Sun **2**	**Good for:** Grand opening, wedding, contracts *Bad for:* Fix house, moving	*Horse*
Mon **3**	**Good for:** Prayer, planting *Bad for:* Grand opening, wedding	*Sheep*
Tue **4**	⊖ **DON'T DO IMPORTANT THINGS** ⊖	*Monkey*
Wed **5**	**Good for:** Grand opening, buy property, wedding *Bad for:* Burial, ground breaking	*Rooster*
Thu **6**	**Good for:** Prayer, burial *Bad for:* Moving, wedding	*Dog*
Fri **7**	**Good for:** Begin mission, school *Bad for:* Ground breaking, wedding	*Pig*
Sat **8**	**Good for:** Prayer, worship *Bad for:* Begin mission, moving	*Rat*
Sun **9**	**Good for:** Worship *Bad for:* Grand opening, ground breaking, wedding	*Ox*
Mon **10**	⊖ **DON'T DO IMPORTANT THINGS** ⊖	*Tiger*
Tue **11**	**Good for:** Contracts, business *Bad for:* Fix house, ground breaking	*Rabbit*
Wed **12**	**Good for:** Prayer, worship *Bad for:* Grand opening, moving	*Dragon*
Thu **13**	⊖ **DON'T DO IMPORTANT THINGS** ⊖	*Snake*
Fri **14**	**Good for:** Prayer, worship *Bad for:* Wedding, ground breaking	*Horse*
Sat **15**	**Good for:** Begin mission, moving, wedding *Bad for:* Lawsuit, funeral	*Sheep*

Day	Activities	Zodiac
Sun 16	**Good for:** Contracts, wedding, grand opening *Bad for: Burial, funeral*	Monkey
Mon 17	**Good for:** Prayer, school *Bad for: Burial, ground breaking*	Rooster
Tue 18	**Good for:** Business, burial *Bad for: Moving, wedding*	Dog
Wed 19	**Good for:** Begin mission, school *Bad for: Ground breaking, burial*	Pig
Thu 20	**Good for:** Prayer, planting *Bad for: Lawsuit, moving*	Rat
Fri 21	**Good for:** Burial, planting *Bad for: Grand opening, wedding*	Ox
Sat 22	⊝ **DON'T DO IMPORTANT THINGS** ⊝	Tiger
Sun 23	**Good for:** Contracts, grand opening, wedding *Bad for: Ground breaking, planting*	Rabbit
Mon 24	**Good for:** Prayer, worship *Bad for: Grand opening, wedding*	Dragon
Tue 25	⊝ **DON'T DO IMPORTANT THINGS** ⊝	Snake
Wed 26	**Good for:** Begin mission, moving *Bad for: Moving, travel*	Horse
Thu 27	**Good for:** Grand opening, wedding *Bad for: Lawsuit, moving*	Sheep
Fri 28	**Good for:** Prayer, worship *Bad for: Burial, grand opening*	Monkey
Sat 29	**Good for:** Prayer, school *Bad for: Burial, ground breaking*	Rooster
Sun 30	**Good for:** Prayer, worship *Bad for: Travel, wedding*	Dog
Mon 31	**Good for:** Begin mission, school *Bad for: Burial, ground breaking, grand opening*	Pig

S	M	T	W	T	F	S
		1	2	3	4	5
6	7	8	9	10	11	12
13	14	15	16	17	18	19
20	21	22	23	24	25	26
27	28	29	30			

June 2010

Unfavorable for:

Day		Unfavorable for:
Tue **1**	**Good for:** Funeral, burial *Bad for: Grand opening, wedding*	*Rat*
Wed **2**	**Good for:** Worship *Bad for: Ground breaking, wedding*	*Ox*
Thu **3**	⊖ **DON'T DO IMPORTANT THINGS** ⊖	*Tiger*
Fri **4**	**Good for:** Business, contracts, wedding *Bad for: Burial, ground breaking*	*Rabbit*
Sat **5**	**Good for:** Prayer, worship *Bad for: Grand opening, moving*	*Dragon*
Sun **6**	**Good for:** Worship *Bad for: Grand opening, ground breaking, wedding*	*Snake*
Mon **7**	⊖ **DON'T DO IMPORTANT THINGS** ⊖	*Horse*
Tue **8**	**Good for:** Planting, worship *Bad for: Begin mission, grand opening*	*Sheep*
Wed **9**	**Good for:** Grand opening, contracts, wedding *Bad for: Lawsuit, moving*	*Monkey*
Thu **10**	**Good for:** Prayer, worship *Bad for: Grand opening, burial*	*Rooster*
Fri **11**	**Good for:** Begin mission, moving, travel *Bad for: Burial, ground breaking*	*Dog*
Sat **12**	**Good for:** Worship, funeral *Bad for: Moving, wedding*	*Pig*
Sun **13**	**Good for:** Prayer, planting *Bad for: Begin mission, fix house, moving*	*Rat*
Mon **14**	**Good for:** Begin mission, business, contracts *Bad for: Fix house, ground breaking*	*Ox*
Tue **15**	⊖ **DON'T DO IMPORTANT THINGS** ⊖	*Tiger*

Wed **16**	⊖ **DON'T DO IMPORTANT THINGS** ⊖	*Rabbit*
Thu **17**	**Good for:** Business, planting ***Bad for:*** *Buy property, fix house*	*Dragon*
Fri **18**	**Good for:** Worship ***Bad for:*** *Ground breaking, wedding*	*Snake*
Sat **19**	⊖ **DON'T DO IMPORTANT THINGS** ⊖	*Horse*
Sun **20**	⊖ **DON'T DO IMPORTANT THINGS** ⊖	*Sheep*
Mon **21**	**Good for:** Begin mission, grand opening, wedding ***Bad for:*** *Lawsuit, moving*	*Monkey*
Tue **22**	**Good for:** Prayer, worship ***Bad for:*** *Grand opening, ground breaking*	*Rooster*
Wed **23**	**Good for:** Prayer, worship ***Bad for:*** *Burial, ground breaking*	*Dog*
Thu **24**	**Good for:** Burial, worship ***Bad for:*** *Grand opening, wedding*	*Pig*
Fri **25**	**Good for:** Planting, school ***Bad for:*** *Grand opening, ground breaking*	*Rat*
Sat **26**	**Good for:** Buy property, grand opening, wedding ***Bad for:*** *Burial, funeral*	*Ox*
Sun **27**	⊖ **DON'T DO IMPORTANT THINGS** ⊖	*Tiger*
Mon **28**	**Good for:** Prayer, worship ***Bad for:*** *Begin mission, grand opening, wedding*	*Rabbit*
Tue **29**	**Good for:** Grand opening, wedding, moving ***Bad for:*** *Planting, ground breaking*	*Dragon*
Wed **30**	**Good for:** Worship ***Bad for:*** *Grand opening, moving*	*Snake*

S	M	T	W	T	F	S
				1	2	3
4	5	6	7	8	9	10
11	12	13	14	15	16	17
18	19	20	21	22	23	24
25	26	27	28	29	30	31

July 2010

Unfavorable for:

Thu **1**	⊖ **DON'T DO IMPORTANT THINGS** ⊖	*Horse*
Fri **2**	**Good for:** Worship **Bad for:** *Fix house, moving*	*Sheep*
Sat **3**	**Good for:** Fix house, ground breaking, wedding **Bad for:** *Lawsuit, moving*	*Monkey*
Sun **4**	**Good for:** Prayer, worship **Bad for:** *Ground breaking, wedding*	*Rooster*
Mon **5**	**Good for:** Grand opening, wedding, contracts **Bad for:** *Burial, funeral*	*Dog*
Tue **6**	**Good for:** Worship **Bad for:** *Wedding, travel*	*Pig*
Wed **7**	**Good for:** Worship **Bad for:** *Grand opening, wedding*	*Rat*
Thu **8**	**Good for:** Begin mission, moving **Bad for:** *Burial, grand opening*	*Ox*
Fri **9**	⊖ **DON'T DO IMPORTANT THINGS** ⊖	*Tiger*
Sat **10**	**Good for:** Worship **Bad for:** *Business, grand opening*	*Rabbit*
Sun **11**	⊖ **DON'T DO IMPORTANT THINGS** ⊖	*Dragon*
Mon **12**	**Good for:** Business, contracts **Bad for:** *Burial, ground breaking*	*Snake*
Tue **13**	**Good for:** Grand opening, wedding, begin mission **Bad for:** *Moving, lawsuit*	*Horse*
Wed **14**	⊖ **DON'T DO IMPORTANT THINGS** ⊖	*Sheep*
Thu **15**	**Good for:** Grand opening, school, fix house **Bad for:** *Burial, funeral*	*Monkey*

100

Day	Details	Zodiac
Fri **16**	**Good for:** Business, buy property, contracts *Bad for: Moving, ground breaking*	*Rooster*
Sat **17**	**Good for:** Worship *Bad for: Grand opening, burial*	*Dog*
Sun **18**	**Good for:** Begin mission, school *Bad for: Burial, ground breaking*	*Pig*
Mon **19**	**Good for:** Burial, ground breaking *Bad for: Moving, wedding*	*Rat*
Tue **20**	**Good for:** Worship, begin mission *Bad for: Ground breaking, wedding*	*Ox*
Wed **21**	⬤ **DON'T DO IMPORTANT THINGS** ⬤	*Tiger*
Thu **22**	**Good for:** Worship *Bad for: Ground breaking, lawsuit*	*Rabbit*
Fri **23**	**Good for:** Worship, prayer *Bad for: Grand opening, wedding*	*Dragon*
Sat **24**	**Good for:** Business, begin mission, fix house *Bad for: Ground breaking, travel*	*Snake*
Sun **25**	**Good for:** Worship *Bad for: Grand opening, moving*	*Horse*
Mon **26**	⬤ **DON'T DO IMPORTANT THINGS** ⬤	*Sheep*
Tue **27**	**Good for:** Burial, fix house, ground breaking *Bad for: Travel, wedding*	*Monkey*
Wed **28**	**Good for:** Grand opening, wedding *Bad for: Lawsuit, moving*	*Rooster*
Thu **29**	**Good for:** Worship *Bad for: Business, grand opening*	*Dog*
Fri **30**	**Good for:** Begin mission, school *Bad for: Burial, ground breaking*	*Pig*
Sat **31**	**Good for:** Ground breaking, burial *Bad for: Grand opening, wedding*	*Rat*

S	M	T	W	T	F	S
1	2	3	4	5	6	7
8	9	10	11	12	13	14
15	16	17	18	19	20	21
22	23	24	25	26	27	28
29	30	31				

August 2010

Unfavorable for:

Sun **1**	**Good for:** Begin mission, moving *Bad for: Wedding, ground breaking*	*Ox*
Mon **2**	⊝ **DON'T DO IMPORTANT THINGS** ⊝	*Tiger*
Tue **3**	**Good for:** Worship *Bad for: Ground breaking, moving*	*Rabbit*
Wed **4**	⊝ **DON'T DO IMPORTANT THINGS** ⊝	*Dragon*
Thu **5**	**Good for:** Fix house, ground breaking *Bad for: Begin mission, wedding*	*Snake*
Fri **6**	⊝ **DON'T DO IMPORTANT THINGS** ⊝	*Horse*
Sat **7**	**Good for:** Prayer, planting *Bad for: Grand opening, wedding*	*Sheep*
Sun **8**	⊝ **DON'T DO IMPORTANT THINGS** ⊝	*Monkey*
Mon **9**	**Good for:** Worship *Bad for: Fix house, ground breaking, wedding*	*Rooster*
Tue **10**	**Good for:** Grand opening, fix house *Bad for: Lawsuit, moving*	*Dog*
Wed **11**	**Good for:** Wedding, grand opening, business *Bad for: Burial, funeral*	*Pig*
Thu **12**	**Good for:** Begin mission, school *Bad for: Burial, ground breaking*	*Rat*
Fri **13**	**Good for:** Burial, business *Bad for: Moving, wedding*	*Ox*
Sat **14**	⊝ **DON'T DO IMPORTANT THINGS** ⊝	*Tiger*
Sun **15**	**Good for:** Burial, ground breaking *Bad for: Begin mission, moving*	*Rabbit*

Day	Good/Bad for	Zodiac
Mon **16**	**Good for:** Begin mission, grand opening *Bad for: Burial, funeral*	*Dragon*
Tue **17**	**Good for:** Prayer, worship *Bad for: Begin mission, grand opening*	*Snake*
Wed **18**	**Good for:** Business, contracts *Bad for: Ground breaking, fix house*	*Horse*
Thu **19**	**Good for:** Fix house, ground breaking *Bad for: Lawsuit, wedding*	*Sheep*
Fri **20**	⊖ **DON'T DO IMPORTANT THINGS** ⊖	*Monkey*
Sat **21**	**Good for:** Wedding, begin mission *Bad for: Funeral, ground breaking*	*Rooster*
Sun **22**	**Good for:** Prayer, worship *Bad for: Ground breaking, wedding*	*Dog*
Mon **23**	**Good for:** Worship *Bad for: Burial, ground breaking*	*Pig*
Tue **24**	**Good for:** School, prayer *Bad for: Ground breaking, planting*	*Rat*
Wed **25**	**Good for:** Worship, burial *Bad for: Moving, fix house*	*Ox*
Thu **26**	⊖ **DON'T DO IMPORTANT THINGS** ⊖	*Tiger*
Fri **27**	**Good for:** Burial, ground breaking *Bad for: Begin mission, grand opening*	*Rabbit*
Sat **28**	**Good for:** Prayer, planting *Bad for: Ground breaking, wedding*	*Dragon*
Sun **29**	**Good for:** Prayer, worship *Bad for: Grand opening, wedding, begin mission*	*Snake*
Mon **30**	**Good for:** Business, contracts, wedding *Bad for: Burial, funeral*	*Horse*
Tue **31**	**Good for:** Fix house, ground breaking *Bad for: Grand opening, travel*	*Sheep*

S	M	T	W	T	F	S
			1	2	3	4
5	6	7	8	9	10	11
12	13	14	15	16	17	18
19	20	21	22	23	24	25
26	27	28	29	30		

September 2010

Unfavorable for:

Date		Unfavorable for:
Wed 1	⊖ **DON'T DO IMPORTANT THINGS** ⊖	*Monkey*
Thu 2	⊖ **DON'T DO IMPORTANT THINGS** ⊖	*Rooster*
Fri 3	**Good for:** Begin mission, school ***Bad for:*** *Grand opening, wedding*	*Dog*
Sat 4	**Good for:** Begin mission, grand opening, wedding ***Bad for:*** *Ground breaking*	*Pig*
Sun 5	**Good for:** Business, grand opening, wedding ***Bad for:*** *Burial, ground breaking*	*Rat*
Mon 6	**Good for:** Worship ***Bad for:*** *Grand opening, wedding*	*Ox*
Tue 7	⊖ **DON'T DO IMPORTANT THINGS** ⊖	*Tiger*
Wed 8	**Good for:** Business, worship ***Bad for:*** *Ground breaking, wedding*	*Rabbit*
Thu 9	**Good for:** Begin mission, ground breaking, moving ***Bad for:*** *Lawsuit, grand opening*	*Dragon*
Fri 10	**Good for:** Prayer, worship ***Bad for:*** *Ground breaking, moving*	*Snake*
Sat 11	**Good for:** Worship ***Bad for:*** *Grand opening, wedding*	*Horse*
Sun 12	**Good for:** Begin mission, grand opening, wedding ***Bad for:*** *Ground breaking, fix house*	*Sheep*
Mon 13	**Good for:** Prayer, worship ***Bad for:*** *Fix house, wedding*	*Monkey*
Tue 14	⊖ **DON'T DO IMPORTANT THINGS** ⊖	*Rooster*
Wed 15	**Good for:** Planting, prayer ***Bad for:*** *Grand opening, wedding, begin mission*	*Dog*

Thu **16**	**Good for:** Business, contracts, wedding *Bad for: Burial, funeral*	Pig
Fri **17**	**Good for:** Business, planting, prayer *Bad for: Lawsuit, moving*	Rat
Sat **18**	**Good for:** Begin mission, grand opening, wedding *Bad for: Burial, ground breaking*	Ox
Sun **19**	⊖ **DON'T DO IMPORTANT THINGS** ⊖	Tiger
Mon **20**	**Good for:** Business, prayer *Bad for: Grand opening, wedding*	Rabbit
Tue **21**	**Good for:** Begin mission, business *Bad for: Fix house, moving*	Dragon
Wed **22**	⊖ **DON'T DO IMPORTANT THINGS** ⊖	Snake
Thu **23**	**Good for:** Worship *Bad for: Moving, wedding*	Horse
Fri **24**	**Good for:** Business, contracts *Bad for: Fix house, ground breaking*	Sheep
Sat **25**	**Good for:** Prayer, worship *Bad for: Begin mission, grand opening*	Monkey
Sun **26**	⊖ **DON'T DO IMPORTANT THINGS** ⊖	Rooster
Mon **27**	**Good for:** Wedding, grand opening, fix house *Bad for: Burial, funeral*	Dog
Tue **28**	**Good for:** Contracts, grand opening, wedding *Bad for: Lawsuit, moving*	Pig
Wed **29**	**Good for:** Prayer, worship *Bad for: Burial, wedding*	Rat
Thu **30**	**Good for:** Begin mission, wedding *Bad for: Burial, ground breaking*	Ox

					1	2
3	4	5	6	7	8	9
10	11	12	13	14	15	16
17	18	19	20	21	22	23
24	25	26	27	28	29	30
31						

October 2010

Unfavorable for:

Day	Details	Unfavorable for
Fri 1	⊖ **DON'T DO IMPORTANT THINGS** ⊖	*Tiger*
Sat 2	**Good for:** Prayer, begin mission *Bad for: Ground breaking, wedding*	*Rabbit*
Sun 3	**Good for:** Begin mission, business *Bad for: Ground breaking, wedding*	*Dragon*
Mon 4	**Good for:** Grand opening, moving *Bad for: Funeral, ground breaking*	*Snake*
Tue 5	**Good for:** Worship *Bad for: Grand opening, wedding*	*Horse*
Wed 6	**Good for:** Prayer, school *Bad for: Grand opening, moving*	*Sheep*
Thu 7	**Good for:** Fix house, funeral *Bad for: Grand opening, travel*	*Monkey*
Fri 8	**Good for:** Begin mission, grand opening, wedding *Bad for: Fix house, moving*	*Rooster*
Sat 9	⊖ **DON'T DO IMPORTANT THINGS** ⊖	*Dog*
Sun 10	**Good for:** Moving, wedding, contracts *Bad for: Burial, funeral*	*Pig*
Mon 11	**Good for:** Contracts, grand opening, wedding *Bad for: Fix house, ground breaking*	*Rat*
Tue 12	**Good for:** Worship *Bad for: Lawsuit, grand opening*	*Ox*
Wed 13	⊖ **DON'T DO IMPORTANT THINGS** ⊖	*Tiger*
Thu 14	**Good for:** Worship, burial *Bad for: Grand opening, wedding*	*Rabbit*
Fri 15	**Good for:** Begin mission, travel *Bad for: Funeral, ground breaking*	*Dragon*

Sat **16**	⊜ **DON'T DO IMPORTANT THINGS** ⊜	*Snake*
Sun **17**	**Good for:** Prayer, worship *Bad for: Grand opening, wedding*	*Horse*
Mon **18**	**Good for:** Prayer, school *Bad for: Fix house, ground breaking*	*Sheep*
Tue **19**	**Good for:** Business, contracts *Bad for: Lawsuit, burial*	*Monkey*
Wed **20**	**Good for:** Begin mission, ground breaking, wedding *Bad for: Burial, funeral*	*Rooster*
Thu **21**	⊜ **DON'T DO IMPORTANT THINGS** ⊜	*Dog*
Fri **22**	**Good for:** Prayer, planting *Bad for: Grand opening, wedding*	*Pig*
Sat **23**	**Good for:** Begin mission, contracts, wedding *Bad for: Fix house, funeral*	*Rat*
Sun **24**	**Good for:** Worship *Bad for: Burial, ground breaking*	*Ox*
Mon **25**	⊜ **DON'T DO IMPORTANT THINGS** ⊜	*Tiger*
Tue **26**	**Good for:** Business, worship *Bad for: Grand opening, wedding*	*Rabbit*
Wed **27**	**Good for:** Begin mission, school *Bad for: Ground breaking, burial*	*Dragon*
Thu **28**	**Good for:** Moving, fix house *Bad for: Ground breaking*	*Snake*
Fri **29**	**Good for:** Grand opening, worship *Bad for: Ground breaking, moving*	*Horse*
Sat **30**	**Good for:** Worship *Bad for: Grand opening, wedding*	*Sheep*
Sun **31**	**Good for:** Business, contracts *Bad for: Wedding, moving*	*Monkey*

S M T W T F S
1 2 3 4 5 6
7 8 9 10 11 12 13
14 15 16 17 18 19 20
21 22 23 24 25 26 27
28 29 30

November 2010

Unfavorable for:

Day	Details	Unfavorable for
Mon 1	**Good for:** Worship ***Bad for:*** *Grand opening, burial, funeral*	*Rooster*
Tue 2	⊖ **DON'T DO IMPORTANT THINGS** ⊖	*Dog*
Wed 3	**Good for:** Prayer, planting ***Bad for:*** *Grand opening, wedding*	*Pig*
Thu 4	**Good for:** Begin mission, grand opening, wedding ***Bad for:*** *Lawsuit*	*Rat*
Fri 5	**Good for:** Business, contracts ***Bad for:*** *Burial, grand opening*	*Ox*
Sat 6	⊖ **DON'T DO IMPORTANT THINGS** ⊖	*Tiger*
Sun 7	**Good for:** Begin mission, school ***Bad for:*** *Fix house, moving*	*Rabbit*
Mon 8	**Good for:** Business, fix house ***Bad for:*** *Travel, wedding*	*Dragon*
Tue 9	**Good for:** Begin mission, travel ***Bad for:*** *Ground breaking, wedding*	*Snake*
Wed 10	**Good for:** Business, grand opening, wedding ***Bad for:*** *Lawsuit, ground breaking*	*Horse*
Thu 11	**Good for:** Worship ***Bad for:*** *Ground breaking, planting*	*Sheep*
Fri 12	**Good for:** Business, contracts, wedding ***Bad for:*** *Funeral, fix house*	*Monkey*
Sat 13	**Good for:** Begin mission, grand opening, wedding ***Bad for:*** *Ground breaking, lawsuit*	*Rooster*
Sun 14	**Good for:** Fix house, moving ***Bad for:*** *Business, buy property*	*Dog*
Mon 15	⊖ **DON'T DO IMPORTANT THINGS** ⊖	*Pig*

Tue **16**	**Good for:** Begin mission, grand opening, wedding *Bad for: Fix house, funeral*	*Rat*
Wed **17**	**Good for:** Business, contracts, grand opening *Bad for: Ground breaking, fix house*	*Ox*
Thu **18**	⊖ **DON'T DO IMPORTANT THINGS** ⊖	*Tiger*
Fri **19**	**Good for:** Prayer, school *Bad for: Ground breaking, burial*	*Rabbit*
Sat **20**	**Good for:** Prayer, worship *Bad for: Grand opening, wedding*	*Dragon*
Sun **21**	**Good for:** Planting, prayer *Bad for: Begin mission, travel*	*Snake*
Mon **22**	**Good for:** Moving, school *Bad for: Fix house, grand opening*	*Horse*
Tue **23**	**Good for:** Worship *Bad for: Grand opening, wedding*	*Sheep*
Wed **24**	**Good for:** Grand opening, wedding, begin mission *Bad for: Burial, funeral*	*Monkey*
Thu **25**	**Good for:** Business, contracts *Bad for: Ground breaking, planting*	*Rooster*
Fri **26**	**Good for:** Wedding, contracts *Bad for: Ground breaking, fix house*	*Dog*
Sat **27**	⊖ **DON'T DO IMPORTANT THINGS** ⊖	*Pig*
Sun **28**	**Good for:** Worship *Bad for: Begin mission, grand opening*	*Rat*
Mon **29**	**Good for:** Begin mission, grand opening, business *Bad for: Ground breaking, lawsuit*	*Ox*
Tue **30**	⊖ **DON'T DO IMPORTANT THINGS** ⊖	*Tiger*

S	M	T	W	T	F	S
			1	2	3	4
5	6	7	8	9	10	11
12	13	14	15	16	17	18
19	20	21	22	23	24	25
26	27	28	29	30	31	

December 2010

Unfavorable for:

Day	Good for / Bad for	Unfavorable for
Wed 1	**Good for:** Begin mission, grand opening, wedding **Bad for:** Burial, ground breaking	*Rabbit*
Thu 2	**Good for:** Prayer, worship **Bad for:** Grand opening, wedding	*Dragon*
Fri 3	**Good for:** Planting, prayer **Bad for:** Fix house, moving	*Snake*
Sat 4	**Good for:** Fix house **Bad for:** Business, buy property	*Horse*
Sun 5	**Good for:** Worship **Bad for:** Grand opening, ground breaking	*Sheep*
Mon 6	**Good for:** Begin mission, grand opening, wedding **Bad for:** Burial, funeral	*Monkey*
Tue 7	**Good for:** Worship **Bad for:** Begin mission, grand opening, wedding	*Rooster*
Wed 8	**Good for:** Buy property, contracts, wedding **Bad for:** Ground breaking, fix house	*Dog*
Thu 9	**Good for:** Burial, ground breaking **Bad for:** Grand opening, travel	*Pig*
Fri 10	⊜ **DON'T DO IMPORTANT THINGS** ⊜	*Rat*
Sat 11	**Good for:** Prayer, worship **Bad for:** Begin mission, fix house, grand opening	*Ox*
Sun 12	⊜ **DON'T DO IMPORTANT THINGS** ⊜	*Tiger*
Mon 13	**Good for:** Planting, prayer **Bad for:** Grand opening, wedding	*Rabbit*
Tue 14	**Good for:** Prayer, worship **Bad for:** Business, contracts	*Dragon*
Wed 15	**Good for:** Worship **Bad for:** Grand opening, ground breaking	*Snake*

Day	Activities	Zodiac
Thu **16**	**Good for:** Travel, begin mission *Bad for: Fix house, ground breaking*	*Horse*
Fri **17**	**Good for:** Business, ground breaking, wedding *Bad for: Funeral, lawsuit*	*Sheep*
Sat **18**	**Good for:** Business, grand opening, wedding *Bad for: Burial, ground breaking*	*Monkey*
Sun **19**	**Good for:** Worship *Bad for: Grand opening, wedding*	*Rooster*
Mon **20**	**Good for:** Begin mission, school *Bad for: Business, buy property*	*Dog*
Tue **21**	⊖ **DON'T DO IMPORTANT THINGS** ⊖	*Pig*
Wed **22**	⊖ **DON'T DO IMPORTANT THINGS** ⊖	*Rat*
Thu **23**	**Good for:** Prayer, worship *Bad for: Buy property, fix house*	*Ox*
Fri **24**	⊖ **DON'T DO IMPORTANT THINGS** ⊖	*Tiger*
Sat **25**	**Good for:** Worship, school *Bad for: Grand opening, ground breaking*	*Rabbit*
Sun **26**	**Good for:** Fix house, ground breaking *Bad for: Wedding, contracts*	*Dragon*
Mon **27**	**Good for:** Worship *Bad for: Ground breaking, wedding*	*Snake*
Tue **28**	**Good for:** Begin mission, travel *Bad for: Grand opening, wedding*	*Horse*
Wed **29**	**Good for:** Business, grand opening, wedding *Bad for: Lawsuit, ground breaking*	*Sheep*
Thu **30**	**Good for:** Begin mission, grand opening, ground breaking *Bad for: Wedding, funeral*	*Monkey*
Fri **31**	**Good for:** Worship *Bad for: Grand opening, wedding*	*Rooster*

S	M	T	W	T	F	S
						1
2	3	4	5	6	7	8
9	10	11	12	13	14	15
16	17	18	19	20	21	22
23	24	25	26	27	28	29
30	31					

January 2011

Unfavorable for:

Day		Unfavorable for
Sat 1	**Good for:** Business, begin mission, wedding *Bad for: Lawsuit, travel*	Dog
Sun 2	**Good for:** Prayer, worship *Bad for: Grand opening, ground breaking*	Pig
Mon 3	⊖ **DON'T DO IMPORTANT THINGS** ⊖	Rat
Tue 4	**Good for:** Planting, prayer *Bad for: Begin mission, grand opening, wedding*	Ox
Wed 5	⊖ **DON'T DO IMPORTANT THINGS** ⊖	Tiger
Thu 6	**Good for:** Business, grand opening, wedding *Bad for: Lawsuit, moving*	Rabbit
Fri 7	**Good for:** Prayer, worship *Bad for: Grand opening, burial*	Dragon
Sat 8	**Good for:** Planting, prayer *Bad for: Begin mission, wedding*	Snake
Sun 9	**Good for:** Burial, ground breaking *Bad for: Lawsuit, grand opening*	Horse
Mon 10	**Good for:** Worship, contracts *Bad for: Ground breaking*	Sheep
Tue 11	**Good for:** Planting, school *Bad for: Grand opening, wedding*	Monkey
Wed 12	**Good for:** Prayer, worship *Bad for: Begin mission, grand opening*	Rooster
Thu 13	**Good for:** Worship *Bad for: Ground breaking, wedding*	Dog
Fri 14	**Good for:** Fix house, business, contracts *Bad for: Burial, ground breaking*	Pig
Sat 15	**Good for:** Begin mission, moving, wedding *Bad for: Lawsuit, funeral*	Rat

Day		Activities	Zodiac
Sun	16	⚊ DON'T DO IMPORTANT THINGS ⚊	Ox
Mon	17	⚊ DON'T DO IMPORTANT THINGS ⚊	Tiger
Tue	18	**Good for:** Grand opening, school, wedding *Bad for: Fix house, burial*	Rabbit
Wed	19	**Good for:** Prayer, worship *Bad for: Grand opening, wedding*	Dragon
Thu	20	**Good for:** Ground breaking, worship *Bad for: Lawsuit, fix house*	Snake
Fri	21	**Good for:** Burial, worship *Bad for: Moving, grand opening*	Horse
Sat	22	⚊ DON'T DO IMPORTANT THINGS ⚊	Sheep
Sun	23	**Good for:** Fix house, travel *Bad for: Begin mission, grand opening*	Monkey
Mon	24	**Good for:** Planting, prayer *Bad for: Lawsuit, moving*	Rooster
Tue	25	**Good for:** Prayer, worship *Bad for: Begin mission, grand opening*	Dog
Wed	26	**Good for:** Begin mission, business, contracts *Bad for: Ground breaking, lawsuit*	Pig
Thu	27	**Good for:** Contracts, wedding *Bad for: Moving, burial*	Rat
Fri	28	⚊ DON'T DO IMPORTANT THINGS ⚊	Ox
Sat	29	⚊ DON'T DO IMPORTANT THINGS ⚊	Tiger
Sun	30	**Good for:** Grand opening, wedding, buy property *Bad for: Lawsuit*	Rabbit
Mon	31	**Good for:** Prayer, worship *Bad for: Begin mission, grand opening, wedding*	Dragon

知足是天賜的財富
奢侈是人為的貧窮

Calligraphy by
Larry Sang

Contentment is natural wealth,
luxury is artificial poverty.

Ten Thousand Year Calendar

Ten-Thousand Year Calendar

	1ST MONTH Wu Yin	2ND MONTH Ji Mao	3RD MONTH Geng Chen	4TH MONTH Xin Si	5TH MONTH Ren Wu	6TH MONTH Gui Wei	
1	2/14 Yi Wei	3/16 Yi Chou	4/14 Jia Wu	5/14 Jia Zi	6/12 Gui Si	7/12 Gui Hai	1
2	2/15 Bing Shen	3/17 Bing Yin	4/15 Yi Wei	5/15 Yi Chou	6/13 Jia Wu	7/13 Jia Zi	2
3	2/16 Ding You	3/18 Ding Mao	4/16 Bing Shen	5/16 Bing Yin	6/14 Yi Wei	7/14 Yi Chou	3
4	2/17 Wu Xu	3/19 Wu Chen	4/17 Ding You	5/17 Ding Mao	6/15 Bing Shen	7/15 Bing Yin	4
5	2/18 Ji Hai	3/20 Ji Si	4/18 Wu Xu	5/18 Wu Chen	6/16 Ding You	7/16 Ding Mao	5
6	2/19 Geng Zi	3/21 Geng Wu	4/19 Ji Hai	5/19 Ji Si	6/17 Wu Xu	7/17 Wu Chen	6
7	2/20 Xin Chou	3/22 Xin Wei	4/20 Geng Zi	5/20 Geng Wu	6/18 Ji Hai	7/18 Ji Si	7
8	2/21 Ren Yin	3/23 Ren Shen	4/21 Xin Chou	5/21 Xin Wei	6/19 Geng Zi	7/19 Geng Wu	8
9	2/22 Gui Mao	3/24 Gui You	4/22 Ren Yin	5/22 Ren Shen	6/20 Xin Chou	7/20 Xin Wei	9
10	2/23 Jia Chen	3/25 Jia Xu	4/23 Gui Mao	5/23 Gui You	6/21 Ren Yin	7/21 Ren Shen	10
11	2/24 Yi Si	3/26 Yi Hai	4/24 Jia Chen	5/24 Jia Xu	6/22 Gui Mao	7/22 Gui You	11
12	2/25 Bing Wu	3/27 Bing Zi	4/25 Yi Si	5/25 Yi Hai	6/23 Jia Chen	7/23 Jia Xu	12
13	2/26 Ding Wei	3/28 Ding Chou	4/26 Bing Wu	5/26 Bing Zi	6/24 Yi Si	7/24 Yi Hai	13
14	2/27 Wu Shen	3/29 Wu Yin	4/27 Ding Wei	5/27 Ding Chou	6/25 Bing Wu	7/25 Bing Zi	14
15	2/28 Ji You	3/30 Ji Mao	4/28 Wu Shen	5/28 Wu Yin	6/26 Ding Wei	7/26 Ding Chou	15
16	3/1 Geng Xu	3/31 Geng Chen	4/29 Ji You	5/29 Ji Mao	6/27 Wu Shen	7/27 Wu Yin	16
17	3/2 Xin Hai	4/1 Xin Si	4/30 Geng Xu	5/30 Geng Chen	6/28 Ji You	7/28 Ji Mao	17
18	3/3 Ren Zi	4/2 Ren Wu	5/1 Xin Hai	5/31 Xin Si	6/29 Geng Xu	7/29 Geng Chen	18
19	3/4 Gui Chou	4/3 Gui Wei	5/2 Ren Zi	6/1 Ren Wu	6/30 Xin Hai	7/30 Xin Si	19
20	3/5 Jia Yin	4/4 Jia Shen	5/3 Gui Chou	6/2 Gui Wei	7/1 Ren Zi	7/31 Ren Wu	20
21	3/6 Yi Mao	4/5 Yi You	5/4 Jia Yin	6/3 Jia Shen	7/2 Gui Chou	8/1 Gui Wei	21
22	3/7 Bing Chen	4/6 Bing Xu	5/5 Yi Mao	6/4 Yi You	7/3 Jia Yin	8/2 Jia Shen	22
23	3/8 Ding Si	4/7 Ding Hai	5/6 Bing Chen	6/5 Bing Xu	7/4 Yi Mao	8/3 Yi You	23
24	3/9 Wu Wu	4/8 Wu Zi	5/7 Ding Si	6/6 Ding Hai	7/5 Bing Chen	8/4 Bing Xu	24
25	3/10 Ji Wei	4/9 Ji Chou	5/8 Wu Wu	6/7 Wu Zi	7/6 Ding Si	8/5 Ding Hai	25
26	3/11 Geng Shen	4/10 Geng Yin	5/9 Ji Wei	6/8 Ji Chou	7/7 Wu Wu	8/6 Wu Zi	26
27	3/12 Xin You	4/11 Xin Mao	5/10 Geng Shen	6/9 Geng Yin	7/8 Ji Wei	8/7 Ji Chou	27
28	3/13 Ren Xu	4/12 Ren Chen	5/11 Xin You	6/10 Xin Mao	7/9 Geng Shen	8/8 Geng Yin	28
29	3/14 Gui Hai	4/13 Gui Si	5/12 Ren Xu	6/11 Ren Chen	7/10 Xin You	8/9 Xin Mao	29
30	3/15 Jia Zi		5/13 Gui Hai		7/11 Ren Xu		30
	2 Black	1 White	9 Purple	8 White	7 Red	6 White	
Jie	Li Chun 2/4 6:42a	Jing Zhi 3/6 12:52a	Qing Ming 4/5 5:55a	Li Xia 5/5 11:29p	Mang Zhong 6/6 3:51a	Xiao Shu 7/7 2:14p	Jie
Qi	Yu Shui 2/19 2:35a	Chun Fen 3/21 1:48a	Gu Yu 4/20 1:07p	Xiao Man 5/21 12:29p	Xia Zhi 6/21 8:35p	Da Shu 7/23 7:28a	Qi

2010

萬年曆

	7TH MONTH Jia Shen	8TH MONTH Yi You	9TH MONTH Bing Xu	10TH MONTH Ding Hai	11TH MONTH Wu Zi	12TH MONTH Ji Chou	
1	8/10 Ren Chen	9/8 Xin You	10/8 Xin Mao	11/6 Geng Shen	2010 - 2011 12/6 Geng Yin	1/4 Ji Wei	1
2	8/11 Gui Si	9/9 Ren Xu	10/9 Ren Chen	11/7 Xin You	12/7 Xin Mao	1/5 Geng Shen	2
3	8/12 Jia Wu	9/10 Gui Hai	10/10 Gui Si	11/8 Ren Xu	12/8 Ren Chen	1/6 Xin You	3
4	8/13 Yi Wei	9/11 Jia Zi	10/11 Jia Wu	11/9 Gui Hai	12/9 Gui Si	1/7 Ren Xu	4
5	8/14 Bing Shen	9/12 Yi Chou	10/12 Yi Wei	11/10 Jia Zi	12/10 Jia Wu	1/8 Gui Hai	5
6	8/15 Ding You	9/13 Bing Yin	10/13 Bing Shen	11/11 Yi Chou	12/11 Yi Wei	1/9 Jia Zi	6
7	8/16 Wu Xu	9/14 Ding Mao	10/14 Ding You	11/12 Bing Yin	12/12 Bing Shen	1/10 Yi Chou	7
8	8/17 Ji Hai	9/15 Wu Chen	10/15 Wu Xu	11/13 Ding Mao	12/13 Ding You	1/11 Bing Yin	8
9	8/18 Geng Zi	9/16 Ji Si	10/16 Ji Hai	11/14 Wu Chen	12/14 Wu Xu	1/12 Ding Mao	9
10	8/19 Xin Chou	9/17 Geng Wu	10/17 Geng Zi	11/15 Ji Si	12/15 Ji Hai	1/13 Wu Chen	10
11	8/20 Ren Yin	9/18 Xin Wei	10/18 Xin Chou	11/16 Geng Wu	12/16 Geng Zi	1/14 Ji Si	11
12	8/21 Gui Mao	9/19 Ren Shen	10/19 Ren Yin	11/17 Xin Wei	12/17 Xin Chou	1/15 Geng Wu	12
13	8/22 Jia Chen	9/20 Gui You	10/20 Gui Mao	11/18 Ren Shen	12/18 Ren Yin	1/16 Xin Wei	13
14	8/23 Yi Si	9/21 Jia Xu	10/21 Jia Chen	11/19 Gui You	12/19 Gui Mao	1/17 Ren Shen	14
15	8/24 Bing Wu	9/22 Yi Hai	10/22 Yi Si	11/20 Jia Xu	12/20 Jia Chen	1/18 Gui You	15
16	8/25 Ding Wei	9/23 Bing Zi	10/23 Bing Wu	11/21 Yi Hai	12/21 Yi Si	1/19 Jia Xu	16
17	8/26 Wu Shen	9/24 Ding Chou	10/24 Ding Wei	11/22 Bing Zi	12/22 Bing Wu	1/20 Yi Hai	17
18	8/27 Ji You	9/25 Wu Yin	10/25 Wu Shen	11/23 Ding Chou	12/23 Ding Wei	1/21 Bing Zi	18
19	8/28 Geng Xu	9/26 Ji Mao	10/26 Ji You	11/24 Wu Yin	12/24 Wu Shen	1/22 Ding Chou	19
20	8/29 Xin Hai	9/27 Geng Chen	10/27 Geng Xu	11/25 Ji Mao	12/25 Ji You	1/23 Wu Yin	20
21	8/30 Ren Zi	9/28 Xin Si	10/28 Xin Hai	11/26 Geng Chen	12/26 Geng Xu	1/24 Ji Mao	21
22	8/31 Gui Chou	9/29 Ren Wu	10/29 Ren Zi	11/27 Xin Si	12/27 Xin Hai	1/25 Geng Chen	22
23	9/1 Jia Yin	9/30 Gui Wei	10/30 Gui Chou	11/28 Ren Wu	12/28 Ren Zi	1/26 Xin Si	23
24	9/2 Yi Mao	10/1 Jia Shen	10/31 Jia Yin	11/29 Gui Wei	12/29 Gui Chou	1/27 Ren Wu	24
25	9/3 Bing Chen	10/2 Yi You	11/1 Yi Mao	11/30 Jia Shen	12/30 Jia Yin	1/28 Gui Wei	25
26	9/4 Ding Si	10/3 Bing Xu	11/2 Bing Chen	12/1 Yi You	12/31 Yi Mao	1/29 Jia Shen	26
27	9/5 Wu Wu	10/4 Ding Hai	11/3 Ding Si	12/2 Bing Xu	1/1 Bing Chen	1/30 Yi You	27
28	9/6 Ji Wei	10/5 Wu Zi	11/4 Wu Wu	12/3 Ding Hai	1/2 Ding Si	1/31 Bing Xu	28
29	9/7 Geng Shen	10/6 Ji Chou	11/5 Ji Wei	12/4 Wu Zi	1/3 Wu Wu	2/1 Ding Hai	29
30		10/7 Geng Yin		12/5 Ji Chou		2/2 Wu Zi	30
	5 Yellow	4 Green	3 Jade	2 Black	1 White	9 Purple	
Jie	Li Qiu 8/7 11:57p	Bai Lu 9/8 2:41a	Han Lu 10/8 6:05p	Li Dong 11/7 9:01p	Da Xue 12/7 1:41p	Xiao Han 1/6 12:50a	Jie
Qi	Chu Shu 8/23 2:24p	Qiu Fen 9/23 11:48a	Shuang Jiang 10/23 8:54p	Xiao Xue 11/22 6:16p	Dong Zhi 12/22 7:29a	Da Han 1/20 6:07p	Qi

AFSI Book Store

The Principles of Feng Shui -Book One

After years of intensive research, experimentation, exploration and teaching of Feng Shui, Master Larry Sang put forth his accumulated knowledge and insights into this book. This book will systematically introduce Feng Shui to its readers. This book is recommended for our Beginning, Intermediate and Advanced Feng Shui classes. Available in both paperback and ebook. $18.75 US

Sang's Luopan

The Luopan is a Chinese compass used in Feng Shui readings. It offers more information for a Feng Shui reading besides the cardinal and inter-cardinal directions. Whereas a Western compass may be used in Feng Shui, a Luopan saves several steps in calculations. The Luopan is 4 inches (10 cm) square. The Luopan is recommended for use in our Feng Shui classes and practice. $50.00 US

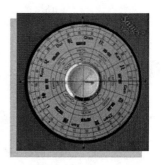

Yi Jing for Love and Marriage

In the journey of life, we often experience times of doubt, confusion and feeling lost. What should we do when facing this type of situation? The Changing Hexagram Divination method can help by prediting what may happen. It can provide guidelines for coping with difficult situations or insight into beneficial ones. This book provides a simple method for the reader to predict the answers to their questions and to help others. Besides resolving confusion and doubt, it also provides a fun hobby for those interested in the ancient art of divination. Use this book as your consultant on Love and Marriage when the need arises!

Available in paperback and ebook. $14.75 US

Ten-Thousand Year Calendar (1882 - 2031)

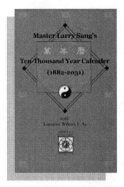

Normally printed in Chinese, but now in English, this handy reference guide is what the Chinese call the Ten-Thousand Year Calendar. This calendar contains information for 150 years, from 1882 to 2031. It gives the annual, monthly, and daily stem and branch, the annual and monthly flying star, as well as the lunar day of the month. It also gives information about the lunar and solar months, the solstices, equinoxes, and the beginning of the four seasons in the Chinese calendar. The Ten-Thousand Year Calendar is used for Feng Shui, Chinese Astrology, Day Selection, and various predictive techniques. 165 Pages.

Available in e-book only. $26.00 US

Feng Shui Facts and Myths

This book is a collection of stories about Feng Shui and Astrology. Master Sang attempts to explain aspects of Feng Shui and Chinese Astrology, as the terms are understood or misunderstood in the West. This book will provide you with deeper information on the Chinese cultural traditions of Feng Shui and Astrology. Available in paperback and ebook.
$16.00 US

Larry Sang's 2010 Chinese Astrology & Feng Shui Guide The Year of the Tiger

Each section explains how to determine the key piece: determining your animal sign; how to read the Feng Shui of your home; and how to read the Day Selection calendar - a valuable day by day indication of favorable and unfavorable activity. Available in paperback and ebook. $14.75 US

COURSE CATALOG

The following is a current list of the courses available from *The American Feng Shui Institute*. Please consult our online catalog for course fees, descriptions and new additions.

FENG SHUI

CLASS	CLASS NAME	PREREQUISITE
FS095	Introduction to Feng Shui	
FS101/OL	Beginning Feng Shui & Online	-
FS102/OL	Intermediate Feng Shui & Online	-
FS201/OL	Advanced Feng Shui & Online	FS102 or FS101/OL
FS205/OL	Advanced Sitting and Facing & Online	FS101 or FS102/OL
FS106/OL	Additional concepts on Sitting & Facing	FS102/OL
FS225	Feng Shui Folk Beliefs	FS201
FS227/OL	Professional Skills for Feng Shui Consultants	FS201
FS231	Feng Shui Yourself & Your Business	FS201
FS235	Symptoms of a House	FS201
FS250	Explanation of Advanced Feng Shui Theories	FS201
FS275	9 Palace Grid and Pie chart Graph Usage & Online	FS201
FS280	Advanced East West Theory	FS201
FS301	Advanced Feng Shui Case Study 1 & 2	FS201
FS303	Advanced Feng Shui Case Study 3 & 4	FS201
FS305/OL	Advanced Feng Shui Case Study 5 & Online	FS201
FS306/OL	Advanced Feng Shui Case Study 6 & Online	FS201
FS307/OL	Advanced Feng Shui Case Study 7 & Online	FS201
FS308/OL	Advanced Feng Shui Case Study 8 & Online	FS201
FS309	Advanced Feng Shui Case Study 9 & 10	FS201
FS311	Advanced Feng Shui Case Study 11	FS201
FS312/OL	Advanced Feng Shui Case Study 12	FS201
FS313/OL	Advanced Feng Shui Case Study 13 & Online	FS201 & AS101
FS314	Advanced Feng Shui Case Study 14	FS201
FS315	Advanced Feng Shui Case Study 15	FS201
FS316	Advanced Feng Shui Case Study 16 & 17	FS201
FS319	Advanced Feng Shui Case Study 19 & 20	FS201
FS321	Advanced Feng Shui Case Study 20 & 21	FS201
FS340/OL	Secrets of the Five Ghosts	FS201
FS341	The Secrets of the "San Ban Gua"	FS201
FS260/OL	Lawsuit Support & Online	FS201 & AS101

FENG SHUI

FS270/OL	The Taisui, Year Breaker, Three Sha & Online	FS201 & AS101
FS350/OL	Feng Shui Day Selection 1 & Online	FS201 & AS101
FS351/OL	Feng Shui Day Selection 2 & Online	FS201 & FS350/OL
FS360/OL	Marriage and Life Partner Selection Online	FS201 & AS101
FS375/OL	Introduction to Yin House Feng Shui	FS201

YI JING

YJ101	Beginning Yi Jing Divination	AS101
YJ102	Yi Jing Coin Divination	AS101
YJ103	Plum Flower Yi Jing Calculation	AS101

CHINESE ASTROLOGY

AS101	Stems and Branches & Online	-
AS102	Four Pillars 1 & 2 (Zi Ping Ba Zi)	AS101 or AS101/OL
AS103	Four Pillars 3 & 4 (Zi Ping Ba Zi)	AS102
AS105	Four Pillars 5 & 6 (Zi Ping Ba Zi)	AS103
AS201A/OL	Beginning Zi Wei Dou Shu, Part 1	AS101
AS201B/OL	Beginning Zi Wei Dou Shu, Part 2	AS201A/OL
AS211/OL	Intermediate Zi Wei Dou Shu	AS201B/OL
AS301A/OL	Advanced Zi Wei Dou Shu, Part 1	AS211/OL
AS301B/OL	Advanced Zi Wei Dou Shu, Part 2	AS201A/OL
AS311/OL	Zi Wei Dou Shu Case Study 1	AS301B/OL
AS313/OL	Zi Wei Dou Shu Case Study 3	AS301B/OL
AS314	Zi Wei Dou Shu Case Study 2 & 4	AS301B/OL

CHINESE ASTROLOGY

CA101/OL	Palm & Face Reading 1 & 2	-
CA102	Palm & Face Reading 3 & 4	CA101 or CA101/OL
CA103	Palm & Face Reading for Health	-
CA121	Introduction to Chinese Medicine	-
CA110	Professional Face Reading	-

CHINESE ASTROLOGY

| CP101 | Introduction to Daode Jing | - |
| CP102 | Feng Shui Yourself | - |

CLASSES AT THE AMERICAN FENG SHUI INSITUTE:

Due to the limited seating capacity, reservations are necessary and seats are on a first come first serve basis. To reserve your seat, a $50.00 US deposit is required and is non-refundable if cancellation by student takes place less than three days before class. Please mail-in check or call us to reserve your seat with a credit card.* Balance is due on the first day of class.

ONLINE CLASSES WITH THE
AMERICAN FENG SHUI INSTITUTE FEATURE:

- Easy navigation
- Self tests at the end of each module
- A discussion board with trained Institute instructors
- Audio clips for prnounciation
- An online discussion board
- An instant feedback final exam

The online classes are self-paced study modules. They are segmented into four, one-week lessons that lead you at your own pace, over the four-week course. You have 60 days to complete the course work.

For more information, please see our website:
www.amfengshui.com

You may register at any time online, by phone or fax:

Tel: (626) 571-2757
Fax: (626) 281-0042

Email: fsinfo@amfengshui.com

American Feng Shui Institute
111 N. Atlantic Blvd. Suite 352
Monterey Park, CA 91754

*Please **DO NOT** email credit card information at this is not a secure method*

AS A STUDENT OF
THE AMERICAN FENG SHUI INSTITUTE:

You will receive a certificate of completion from the American Feng Shui Institute, for the Beginning/Intermediate and Advanced Feng Shui Classes. Please do not confuse this certification as licensing, as there are no requirements for practitioner at this time.

As a student of the Institute, we are available to assist you with your studies. We have an online Bulletin Board for questions and answers, featuring a topic search. You will obtrain access to the Bulletin Board upon completion of the Advanced Feng Shui class. Due to the complexity of the courses, graduates may repeat in the classroom that you have already taken, for $45.00 US per day, pending available seats. Please see our online course catalog for the most current course offerings.

CANCELLATION AND REFUND POLICY:

All institutional charges shall be returned to the registrant less a $50.00 US cancellation fee, if cancellation notice is received prior to or on the first day of instruction. Any notification of withdrawal or cancellation and any request for a refund are required to be made in writing.

Refunds shall be made within thirty (30) days of receipt of the withdrawal or cancellation notice and refund request.

The institute does not participate in the Student Tuition Recovery Fund (STRF). We are registered with the State of California. Registration means we have met certain minimum standards imposed by the state for registered schools on the basis of our written application to the state. Registration does not mean we have met all of the more extensive standards required by the state for schools that are approved to operate or license or that the state has verified the information we submitted with our registration form.

Thank You